HOPES *and* DREAMS

HOPES *and* DREAMS

THE

STORY OF

BARACK OBAMA

STEVE DOUGHERTY

Photo Editor – Hal Buell

BLACK DOG
& LEVENTHAL
PUBLISHERS
NEW YORK

Copyright © 2007 by Black Dog & Leventhal Publishers, Inc.

All rights reserved. No part of this book, either text or illustration, may be used
or reproduced in any form without the prior written permission from the publisher.

Published by Black Dog & Leventhal Publishers, Inc.
151 West 19th Street
New York, NY 10011

Research Assistant: Eva O. Dougherty

Book Design: Sheila Hart Design, Inc.

Photo credits can be found on page 128

ISBN-10: 1-57912-756-8
ISBN-13: 978-1-57912-756-5

h g f e d c b a

Printed in the United States of America

CONTENTS

HOPES *and* DREAMS

OBAMAMANIA

Before he formally launched his campaign for his party's nomination, seeking to become the first black president in American history, Obama—speaking to reporters after winning his 2004 Senate race (above right); celebrating his victory (above) with wife, Michelle, and daughters, Malia and Sasha; and on a campaign flight (right)—rallied Democrats to what he called his "new politics of hope."

1

I really tried to get Bono this weekend," Iowa senator Tom Harkin tells the cheering crowd at his annual Harkin Steak Fry at the Warren County Fairgrounds in Indianola, Iowa. "I settled for the second-biggest rock star in America."

With that, the headline attraction—a brown-eyed handsome man, Usher-smooth and lithe and lean as Justin Timberlake—takes the stage to giddy applause. But the swooning fans aren't going ga-ga just because Barack Obama has won more Grammy Awards (one) than Jimi Hendrix and Bob Marley combined (zero). He's getting the Elvis treatment simply because, as one fan, a young Republican named Veronica Czastkiewicz who drove three hours to catch his act, put it, "Barack's attitude is awesome. He's the only Democrat I'd vote for."

Ever since he wowed the world at the 2004 Democratic convention, won election to the U.S. Senate by a landslide that year, and then by tireless campaigning and the sheer force of his star power helped his party win back both houses of Congress in the 2006 midterm elections, his fans couldn't resist comparing him to the supernovas of rock. "We originally scheduled the Rolling

"There is not a liberal America and a conservative America. There is the United States of America."

BARACK OBAMA

In his star-making speech nominating John Kerry (with Kerry's wife, Teresa, and John Edwards, above right) at the 2004 Democratic Convention, Obama (with Michelle, right) first used the phrase that is the title of his best-selling book *The Audacity of Hope*. "In the end, that is God's greatest gift to us, the bedrock of this nation; the belief in things not seen; the belief that there are better days ahead."

Stones for this party," New Hampshire governor John Lynch told a crowded hall of Barack-and-rollers at a rally in Manchester to celebrate the Democrats' November election victories. "But we cancelled them when we realized that Senator Obama would sell more tickets."

The sold-out rally—and a second appearance in Portsmouth, New Hampshire, where he signed copies of his Oprah-endorsed best

Long-shot hopes are nothing new for Obama (left), a Chicago White Sox fan who celebrates at a rally in 2005, the year the perennial losers won their first World Series since 1917; he campaigns with vice presidential candidate John Edwards and Illinois senator Dick Durbin in 2004 (top left); Obama (above) stands in a Capitol Hill elevator after casting his vote on the nomination of Samuel Alito Jr. for Supreme Court justice in 2006.

seller, *The Audacity of Hope* (he won his 2006 Grammy for Best Spoken Word Album, beating out fellow nominee Bob Dylan, among others, for his audiobook reading of his memoir, *Dreams from My Father,* first published in 1995)—attracted 2,500 people and the kind of media attention more likely to be found at the launch of a Stones tour than at a post-election Granite State political event. Some 150 members of the press, including sixty reporters and twenty-two

TV camera crews, covered Obama's visit to a state that happens to be the site of 2008's first presidential primary.

It was a scene repeated at an earlier series of stops around the country before the midterm elections as Obama launched a book tour that had all the trappings of something quite different.

"Sometimes a book tour is more than just a book tour," a former aide to

Vice President Al Gore slyly noted as the author Obama appeared at signings in Chicago where a woman shouted "Obama for president!" as the senator arrived at a bookstore at 8:30 a.m. for the first of three signings that day and in San Rafael, California, where an enterprising vendor did a brisk business selling homemade "Obama for President" buttons outside the Marin Civic Center while 1,200 people turned out to hear him speak and wait in long lines to have him sign copies of *The Audacity of Hope.* The following day he was in Seattle where the largest single crowd on the tour, 2,500 people, attended a signing at Bellevue Community College and where

> ## "Our vision of America is not one where a big government runs our lives; it's one that gives every American the opportunity to make the most of their lives."
>
> BARACK OBAMA

audience members held up the then-current issue of *Time* magazine with his face on the cover along with the words "Why Barack Obama Could Be the Next President."

"Senator Obama," the former aide said, "appears to be using the book to really test presidential winds."

And so he was. Just three months later, on the morning after what would have been Martin Luther King Jr.'s seventy-eighth birthday, Obama filed papers with the Federal Election Commission, the first

Widely known in his homestate as an effective and innovative legislator during his seven years in the Illinois State Senate, Obama (inset) speaks at a 2005 Building Trades conference in Washington; and talks before the Chicago Council on Foreign Affairs in November 2006.

Obama speaks to the Chicago Council on Foreign Affairs in November 2005, calling for a reduction of troops in Iraq and criticizing the Bush adminstration for questioning the patriotism of those who speak against the war.

step in his quest to become the first black president in American history.

"The decisions that have been made in Washington these past six years, and the problems that have been ignored, have put our country in a precarious place," he

said in a videotaped message to supporters on January 16, 2007, explaining why he was entering the race. Citing voters' jitters about everything from their jobs to jihad and a "tragic and costly war that should never have been waged," Obama called for a new kind of politics to replace the present way of doing business in Washington where things are so "bitter and partisan, so gummed-up by money and influence," he said, "that we can't tackle the big problems that demand solutions."

In New Hampshire, two months before he filed Federal Election Commission papers, Obama's fans already seemed psyched for him to get in the race. Looking dapper and at ease in an open-collar white shirt and a black jacket and speaking in his smooth and rich baritone, Obama was greeted by a sustained fusillade of camera flashes and

> ## "It's just not my style to go out of my way to offend people or be controversial just for the sake of being controversial. That's offensive and counterproductive. It makes people feel defensive and more resistant to changes."
>
> BARACK OBAMA

standing ovations as he called for universal health care, energy independence, an effective policy to stem global warming, and an end to loud and uncivil, Limbaugh-like public discourse. "We've come to be consumed by a 24-hour, slash-and-burn, negative-ad, bickering, small-minded politics that doesn't move us forward," he said

Angered by the Bush administration's reponse to Hurricane Katrina, Obama (at a Habitat for Humanity project in New Orleans in July 2006, right), said the government "was so detached from the realities of inner-city life in New Orleans . . . they couldn't conceive of the notion that [residents] couldn't load up their SUVs . . . and drive off to a hotel with a credit card." Below Obama listens during an October 2006 campaign rally for Ohio gubernatorial candidate Ted Strickland.

in Portsmouth, aiming his critique at both Republicans and his own party as they glowered across a gaping, ever-widening partisan gulf. "Sometimes one side is up, and the other side is down. But there's no sense that they are coming together in a common-sense, practical, nonideological way to solve the problems that we face."

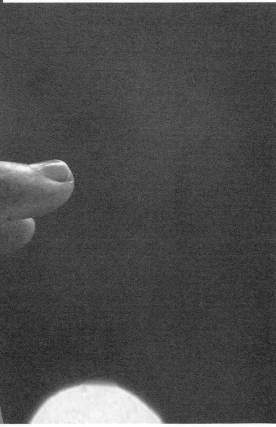

"What's hard, what's risky, what's truly audacious, is to hope."

BARACK OBAMA

The call to overcome the great American cultural and partisan divide is a central theme of both his book *The Audacity of Hope* and his campaign. In times of trouble, when despair and anger may seem the only alternatives, he said in keeping with the book's campaign-ready message, "what's hard, what's risky, what's truly audacious, is to hope."

Obama, whose early and eloquent speeches against the war in Iraq (the looming invasion, he said presciently in 2002, was an ill-conceived venture that would "require a U.S. occupation of undetermined length,

"Run, Barack, run. Barack Obama should run for president. He should run first for the good of his party. It would demoralize the Democrats to go through a long primary season with the most exciting figure in the party looming off in the distance like some unapproachable dream."

DAVID BROOKS, *THE NEW YORK TIMES*

at undetermined cost, with undetermined consequences") lifted the then-obscure Illinois legislator to statewide prominence and paved the way for his march to the Senate, also renewed his call for the redeployment of American troops in Iraq. "We can't just waste our most precious resource—our young men and women," he told the crowd in Portsmouth. The words prompted one listener, a Republican whose son recently returned from his second tour of duty, to tell a reporter, "If he runs [he didn't need to say for what], I'll help."

"He had the true spirit we're looking for," said one member of the Manchester audience who was reminded not of a rock star but of one of an earlier generation's most revered political figures. "I haven't been so excited by someone since JFK when he was campaigning when I was ten years old."

"I've never seen anything like it," echoed a former New Hampshire lawmaker who, as he watched Obama electrify a crowd of normally subdued Democratic Party supporters, thought of the Kennedy to whom Obama is most frequently likened. "A lot of people have compared it to the days when Bobby Kennedy was running for president. I don't think we've seen it since."

Jack or Bobby: to be equated with either is heady stuff for any politician but especially a first-term senator with presidential ambitions. Obama's youth, energy and idealism, not to mention his athletic good looks, have inspired memories of—and comparisons to—both brothers.

"I have no interest in being the un-Hillary," said Obama, whose early opposition to what he calls "the fiasco in Iraq" gained him the support of many Democrats angered by his campaign rival's long-stated support for the war. Even so, he said of Hillary Clinton (with Obama in July 2006), "I think she'd be a capable president."

After all thirty-four presidents to come before him—from the jowly, wooden-toothed father of the country to JFK's immediate predecessor (many said "I Like Ike" but no one ever said Eisenhower was hot)—Jack Kennedy was the first White House rock star, a blast of photogenic, full-color, high-res Hyannis sex appeal.

In Manchester, Obama echoed President Kennedy's call for a New Frontier: "America is ready to turn the page," he said. "America is ready for a new set of challenges. This is our time. A new generation is prepared to lead."

But it is the dead president's younger brother who, like Obama, was a witty, eloquent, dashing, and politically progressive, forty-something freshman junior senator from a large northern industrial state when he ran for president in 1968, to whom Barack is most frequently compared. Bobby Kennedy, who sat at the same desk Obama was assigned when he first sat in the Senate chamber and who was sworn in on January 4, 1965, forty years to the day before his political descendant, launched his quest as the electorate was despairing under the rising death count of a badly conceived and ill-defined, no-end-in-sight war and longed for a return to JFK's Camelot, the brief, however illusory, flowering of optimism that preceded the bitter divisiveness and culture wars that are still with us.

Perhaps realizing the risks involved—the road to political glory is littered with

"Barack represents change and hope," a former Clinton White House political director said of Obama, here talking on a cell phone outside the Senate chamber in April 2006. "There are moments in our country—1960 was one of them—when people are looking for more and are willing to take a chance on [a candidate's potential for] greatness."

nearly as many supposedly Kennedy-esque political stars (Dan Quayle, Jack Kemp anyone? Paging John Edwards!) as Fab Fours and Fives whose sure-thing route to rock stardom ended the moment they were cast as

---

"Everywhere he goes, people want him to run for president, especially in Iowa, cradle of presidential contenders. Around here, they're even naming babies after him."

TERRY MORAN, ABC'S *NIGHTLINE*, DURING HIS PROFILE OF OBAMA

---

the next Beatles—Obama is wise not to fit himself for the Kennedy mantle. Even so, he frequently cites Bobby Kennedy as one of his political heroes, along with other American martyrs JFK, Abraham Lincoln, and Martin Luther King Jr. (In a sad irony, the fortieth anniversary of King's and RFK's deaths by assassins' bullets will be observed at the height of the 2008 presidential election campaign. And reportedly, Obama's wife, Michelle, cited her fears for her husband's security when she argued initially against his running.)

"I was only seven when Bobby Kennedy died," Obama said in an address during the Robert F. Kennedy Human Rights Award Ceremony in Washington in 2005, when Kennedy would have celebrated his eightieth birthday. "I knew him only as an icon."

And yet, when Obama invokes Kennedy in his speeches, he sounds as if he could be reading a passage from his own book. "In a nation torn by war and divided against itself," he said in tribute to RFK, "he was able to look us in the eye and tell us that no matter . . . how persistent the poverty or the racism, no matter how far adrift America strayed, hope would come again."

Like Kennedy, Obama had been a celebrated figure and a beacon of hope for his party—and his country, or so his and Bobby's ardent supporters attest—before he first stepped foot into the Senate chamber and took a seat at his predecessor's desk to become the upper house's third black senator since Reconstruction—and its sole, current African American member.

"He's the star. He is in such demand. He's in greater demand than any other person that we have to offer."

SEN. CHARLES SCHUMER

Obama "is the most galvanizing leader to come out of either party in at least a decade," said Ben Affleck. Among other celeb Obamamaniacs are Tom Cruise and Katie Holmes (with Michelle Obama, left), George Clooney (above), and Bono (right); the Obamas attend the 2005 NAACP Image Awards (top right).

"I miss them terribly and miss Michelle terribly," Obama (with his family in March 2004) said of life on the campaign trail. "I'm just blessed that Michelle is so good with the children and so well organized that she's really been able to take care of home base."

"That would be my favorite guy. . . I would hope that he would run for president."

OPRAH WINFREY

His election victory in November 2004 ignited the near-hysteria known as Obamamania that his supporters hope will carry him all the way to the White House. When he and his wife caught a screening of the film *Ray* at a theater near his home in Hyde Park, on the South Side of Chicago, shortly after the election, audience members clapped and cheered as he took his seat. Mobbed by the media and by passersby on the streets of Chicago and Washington where fans of all ages and ethnic stripes shouted his name, clapped him on the back, and asked him for autographs and to pose for snapshots, Obama found himself at the center of the kind of adulation usually reserved for sports heroes, or movie and—of course—rock stars. Swooning press reports led a waggish *Chicago Reader* writer to note that "No Chicago pol has heard this kind of flattery since an alderman compared Richard J. Daley to Jesus Christ."

Appearances on innumerable talk shows and magazine covers spread his image throughout the land, and his place in the pop firmament was confirmed in an episode of *Will & Grace* when Grace dreamed she showered with the man whom she said was "Barack-ing my world!"

"I'm so overexposed I make Paris Hilton look like a recluse," the senator-elect quipped at the Gridiron Club Dinner in December 2004. "I figure there's nowhere to go from here but down, so tonight I'm announcing my retirement from the United States Senate."

Even before he took the oath of office the following month, out-of-power Democrats—with the words of Obama's stirring convention speech from the summer before still ringing in their ears and tallies of his landslide victory fresh in their minds (he won over 70 percent of the vote in a state where the electorate is only 15 percent black)—began fantasizing about getting him to run in 2008, if not for president, at least vice president. While *Newsweek* termed such talk "almost comically premature for an incoming senator," the magazine also pointed out that Obama, then forty-three, was "the same age JFK was when he was elected president."

A few short years before, the notion that Obama would be "the man . . . more and more people are saying could be America's

first black president," as the host introduced him on *Larry King Live* last October, would not have seemed comical; it simply wouldn't have crossed anyone's mind, least of all Obama's. "Oprah herself wants him to run!" rang out King in near-endorsement.

In *The Audacity of Hope*, Obama recalls that when he attended his first Democratic Convention, in Los Angeles in 2000, he was at the nadir of his political career. Three years after being elected to the Illinois state senate, he made what he now concedes was a hasty and ill-advised attempt to run for Congress in 1999. Critics called it a disaster.

Running to unseat Bobby Rush, a former Black Panther Party member and four-term congressman who enjoyed wide popularity in his overwhelmingly black South Side district in Chicago, Obama endured thinly veiled suggestions that his light-colored skin, his Columbia University and Harvard Law School education, his work as a lawyer and constitutional law professor and his biracial lineage—no descendant of slaves, his father was a government official from Kenya, his mother a Kansas-born WASP—meant that he was elitist and not "black enough" to relate to the lives and needs of the constituents. Rush trounced him by a two-to-one margin in the primary, and Obama retreated to his law practice at a small civil rights firm in Chicago that, he'd "left unattended during the campaign (a neglect that had left [him] more or less broke)."

Just how broke he spells out in his book, describing how when he landed in L.A. for the convention after being cajoled by friends to attend ("Although they didn't say this at the time," he writes, "I suspect they saw a trip to the convention as a bit of useful therapy for me, on the theory that the best thing to do after getting thrown off a horse is to get back on right away"), his American Express card was rejected at the Hertz counter. "After half an hour on the phone, a kindhearted supervisor at American Express authorized the car rental," he writes. "But the episode served as an omen of things to come." Without credentials as a delegate and no floor passes available, he ended up watching the proceedings on televisions set up inside the Staples Center. He left the convention without witnessing the coronation of Al Gore as the Democratic standard-bearer. And he left with scant hope for the future of his political career.

The memory of that experience, and of the electoral slapdown that preceded it, left him with an indelible "sense of how fleeting fame is." It was, he writes, "the sort of drubbing that awakens you to the fact that life is not obliged to work out as you'd planned."

It equipped him to see the foolishness of believing what he calls "the hyperbole" lavished upon him in the wake of his rousing

"Dick Cheney and Donald Rumsfeld have an awful lot of experience."

OBAMA, ON THOSE WHO QUESTION
HIS QUALIFICATIONS FOR HIGHER OFFICE.

speech at that other, happier convention four years later and following his election victory in 2004. "It was my first day in the [Senate office] building," he writes of a press conference he held on the day before his swearing-in 2005. "I had not taken a single vote, had not introduced a single

bill—indeed I had not even sat down at my desk—when a very earnest reporter raised his hand and asked, 'Senator Obama, what is your place in history?'

"Even some of the other reporters had to laugh."

No one was laughing two years later as he answered the drumbeat of supporters calling upon him to launch his candidacy and take his place in history. There were, however, plenty who scoffed that Obama was too young, too inexperienced, and, yes, too black to win in 2008.

While supporters like Illinois Senate President Emil Jones Jr. touted Obama's color-blind appeal by describing encounters like the one he had during the 2004 U.S. Senate campaign with an eighty-six-year-old downstate white woman who said, "I hope I live long enough because this young man's going to be president and I want to be able to vote for him!", *Chicago Sun-Times* columnist Laura Washington quoted her uncle Leland "Sugar" Cain, who said he was a fan of Obama's but doesn't think whites will elect him president. "When it's time to go into the voting booth," Cain told his niece, "they're not going to pull that lever."

New York magazine writer John Heilemann agreed, but argued that race is not the issue. "Obamamaniacs must be smoking something," he quipped. "For all his promise, Obama is basically an empty vessel, with vulnerabilities that have been obscured by his blinding, meteoric ascent."

Like a rock critic puncturing the bubble of the biggest, best-selling rock star's most popular hit, Heilemann belittled oft-heard comparisons of Obama to Bobby Kennedy, saying the differences between them "are many, beginning with the length and depth

28

A member of the Trinity United Church of Christ in Chicago who keeps a Bible in his car, Obama (in a prayerful moment at his church in 2004) has never been a Muslim, as some Rightist talk-radio critics have rumored.

of their résumés. . . . Obama's . . . pales by comparison."

"The excitement he's generated isn't issue-based: it's stylistic," wrote Heilemann, who wondered "how well this brand of popularity will hold up when voters learn more about him . . . such as the fact that he's a smoker."

Heilemann meant cigarettes (Obama, trying to quit, is down to puffing three a day), but when Jay Leno asked him in December 2006 if he smoked, he was talking not about Marlboros but about pot, which Obama had admitted to in *Dreams*

from My Father, a searingly honest and soul-searching memoir written years before he ever considered a political career. Little noticed when it was first published in 1995, it spent a year on the *New York Times* best-seller list when it was reissued in the wake of his political success in 2004. In a preface to the new edition he said that he would not

While he has cosponsored many bills with Republicans as a minority party member in both the Illinois and U.S. Senates, Obama (at his office on Capitol Hill in 2006, above, and with Karl Rove, right) decries Rove's polarizing tactics. At left, Obama speaks at a Summer Intern Town Hall meeting in Washington, 2006.

"In this new economy, teaching our kids just enough so that they can get through Dick and Jane isn't going to cut it."

BARACK OBAMA

"tell the story much differently today than I did ten years ago, even if certain passages have proven to be inconvenient politically."

"Not recently—this was in high school," Obama said in response to Leno's question.

"Did you inhale?" Leno said, alluding to Bill Clinton's famous dodge.

"That was the point," Obama said.

A group of pundits and political analysts quoted in a January 3, 2007, *Washington Post* story said they believe that Obama's disarming candor made it a

dead issue—"Americans have an appetite for redemption," said one Republican consultant. "Who's going to cast the first stone?" asked a Democratic counterpart.

"I am suspicious of hype."

BARACK OBAMA

Obama didn't excise the passages about drug use from his book—he also said that he tried cocaine as well—because, perhaps, as he said during his Senate campaign, he felt it was important for "young people who are already in circumstances far more difficult than mine [were] to know that you can make mistakes and still recover.

"At this stage in my life," he said, "my life is an open book, literally and figuratively. Voters can make a judgment as to whether dumb things that I did when I was a teenager are relevant to the work that I've done since that time."

One conundrum Obama faces is as inescapable as it is impossible to measure for its effect on voters—his name. In *The Audacity of Hope*, he recounts a meeting with a media consultant to discuss his political future. "As it happened, the lunch was scheduled for late September 2001.

"'You realize, don't you, that the political dynamics have changed,'" the consultant said. "We both looked down at the newspaper beside him," Obama writes. "There on the front page was Osama bin Laden.

"'Hell of a thing, isn't it? . . . You can't change your name, of course. Voters are suspicious of that kind of thing. Maybe if you were at the start of your career, you know, you could use a nickname or something. But now . . .'"

Name recognition for any politician is the coin of the realm, but for Obama it seemed a curse. He despaired for a time, imagining it signaled the end of his political career. "I began feeling," he writes, "the way I imagine an actor or athlete must feel when, after years of commitment to a particular dream, after years of waiting tables between auditions or scratching out hits in the minor leagues, he realizes that he's gone just about as far as talent or fortune will take him."

After seriously considering abandoning politics for a "calmer, more stable, and better-paying existence," he writes, "at some point I arrived at acceptance—of my limits, and, in a way, my mortality . . . And it was this acceptance, I think, that allowed me to come up with the thoroughly cockeyed idea of running for the United States Senate."

His supporters can point to it as a testament to his character that he saw the name he inherited from his father, Barack Hussein Obama—triply toxic as it would become with the coming of both Saddam and Borat—as just another obstacle to overcome in pursuit of his own "particular dream." (While Obama seldom if ever uses the middle name, he apparently has instructed his staff to be forthright about it. When a reporter called his office in Washington last year and gingerly asked the correct spelling of the senator's middle name, a staffer said simply, "Like the dictator.")

As deftly as he has managed to defuse the jarring associations attached to his name—Barack means "blessed" in Swahili, he tells audiences; and he invariably gets laughs when

While Obama (in his Senate office, top) relies on staff to handle scheduling and other nuts-and-bolts campaign needs, his closest adviser is himself. "In terms of what's important to the country," he said, "I think my instincts are good. I trust them." At right, Obama prepares for an appearance on his friend Oprah Winfrey's television show in 2006.

he says that people are always hearing Obama as "Alabama" or "Yo Mama"—it has dogged him steadily. Jan Schakowsky, a member of Illinois's congressional delegation has said that when President Bush glimpsed her Obama button during a White House visit in 2004, "He jumped back, almost literally. And I knew what he was thinking. So I reassured him it was Obama, with a 'b'."

Schakowsky explained that Obama was a Chicagoan running for the U.S. Senate.

"Well, I don't know him," Bush said.

"But you will, Mr. President," she replied.

"He's ready. Why wait? Obama '08."

BUMPER STICKER SEEN ALL OVER WASHINGTON, D.C.

"[L]et's face it," Obama said as he began the speech that electrified the 2004 Democratic Convention and that can still inspire the tears of believers, even on the written page, "my presence on this stage is pretty unlikely. My father was a foreign student, born and raised in a small village in Kenya. He grew up herding goats, went to school in a tin-roof shack. His father, my grandfather, was a cook, a domestic servant. . . . Through hard work and perseverance my father got a scholarship to study in a magical place, America, which stood as a beacon of freedom and opportunity to so many who had come before. While studying here, my father met my mother. She was born in a town on the other side of the world, in Kansas . . . My parents shared not only an improbable love; they shared an abiding faith in the possibilities of this nation. They would give

Obama stands at George W. Bush's side after the president signed into law the Federal Funding Accountability and Transparency Act of 2006, a bill cosponsored by Obama and Sen. Tom Coburn, a Republican from Oklahoma.

me an African name, Barack, or 'blessed,' believing that in a tolerant America your name is no barrier to success . . . I stand here knowing that my story is part of the larger American story, that I owe a debt to all of those who came before me, and that, in no other country on earth is my story even possible."

Now he stands on an even larger stage. And Obama's story—of how, as he likes to say, "a tall, skinny kid with big ears," who came from nowhere in the continental United States, who grew up in Hawaii, forever an outsider, a black kid abandoned at age two by his father and, for long periods, his mother, raised by her parents in a white neighborhood and looked at askance by all of a more definable hue and tribe, who struggled mightily to find an identity and a purpose in life, who never really got to know his father until he was in his twenties and stood by his unmarked grave in a dusty African village, has risen to become a candidate for president of the United States and a voice whose call for a union undivided by liberal and conservative, red state and blue, or black and white, springs from his own struggles to find a way to unite his own divided heart—seems all the more unlikely.

YOUNG BARRY

"Come to us, Obama!" crowds waving American flags chanted in Kisumu (right) in 2006 when Obama was also welcomed to his late father's home by villagers in Kogelo (top right) and visited with his step-grandmother, Sarah Hussein Onyango Obama (above).

2

The first time he arrived in Kenya, in 1987 as a twenty-six-year-old Chicago community organizer preparing to enter Harvard Law School, Barack Obama landed at the airport to find that his luggage had been lost en route and he roared—literally—into Nairobi in an aunt's beat-up Volkswagen Beetle with a knocking engine and no muffler.

Later, on his way to his ancestral village of Kogelo, in rural western Kenya—the land immortalized in Hemingway's *Green Hills of Africa*—he took an all-night train to the town of Kisumu and rode from there for hours in an overcrowded and rickety jitney-like matatu with bald tires and few seats. On his lap during the bumpy ride were his half sister Auma, a squealing baby that a stranger asked him to hold, and a basket full of yams. It was not exactly as he had often fantasized his visit to the land of his father—as a "homecoming . . . clouds lifting, old demons fleeing, the earth trembling as ancestors rose up in celebration."

Nineteen years later, that surreal vision seemed to come true before his eyes. When Obama, his wife—Michelle—and their two daughters, Malia and Sasha, landed at

"There's a core decency to the American people that doesn't get enough attention."

BARACK OBAMA

Nairobi's Kenyatta International Airport in the summer of 2006, the U.S. ambassador met their plane, and they were whisked past a throng of waiting reporters and ferried into town in a twelve-car motorcade.

Rapturous crowds of Kenyans wearing T-shirts emblazoned with his name and likeness chanted "Come to us, Obama!" as he visited a memorial at the site of the U.S. embassy bombing in Nairobi.

Skipping the all-night train ride, Obama and his family flew to Kisumu where thousands lined the route to Kogelo, many climbing trees for a better view of the motorcade carrying the American that the local Luo tribespeople loudly claimed as their own. "He's our brother," said one. "He's our son."

In Kogelo, the tiny village where Obama's father and grandfather are buried side by side and where the octogenarian Luo he calls "Granny" still lives, crowds chanted his name, a tribal singer sang his praises, and children sang songs they had composed in his honor. A villager offered him a present "to signify our appreciation"—a three-year-old goat led on a tattered rope leash. "It is very fat," he said, "and very sweet." Obama politely declined and shared a meal of chicken, porridge, and cabbage with his wife and kids, Auma—who acted as interpreter for their Granny, who spoke only Luo—and other relatives.

"Even though I had grown up on the other side of the world," Obama said to villagers of his visit nineteen years before, "I felt the spirit among the people who told me that I belonged."

He had embarked on that journey uneasily, however. He was, he wrote in *Dreams from My Father* (the literary memoir that chronicles his coming of age), "a Westerner not entirely at home in the West, an African on his way to a land full of strangers."

Once there, however, he began to feel the sense of transformation that friends back home had described after their first visits to Africa. "For a span of weeks or months," he wrote, "you could experience the freedom that comes from not feeling watched, the freedom of believing that your hair grows as it's supposed to grow and that your rump sways the way a rump is supposed to sway . . . Here the world was black, and so you were just you."

Until that maiden voyage to Africa, a rite of passage that helped him reconcile the world he grew up in and the world of a father he never really knew, he endured a long and often-painful struggle to understand who he truly was.

It was, he would recall, "a ten-year-old's nightmare." It was 1971, and he had just been introduced to the classroom on his first day of school at Honolulu's Punahou

School by a kindly teacher with the nice name of Miss Hefty, who heard giggles when she used his full name.

"I thought your name was Barry," said a boy he'd met when his grandfather escorted him to school that morning.

"Barack is such a beautiful name," said Miss Hefty, who had lived in Kenya herself and had been delighted to learn that the new boy's father was Kenyan. "It's such a magnificent country. Do you know what tribe your father is from?"

Living in a two-bedroom apartment on the tenth floor of a building in one of the less-fashionable neighborhoods in glitzy Honolulu (left), Obama was admitted to the elite Punahou School (below right and left) at age ten after his grandfather's boss, an alumnus, used his clout to help get him in.

"I found that I've never learned anything from refusing to listen to other people or refusing to engage in conversation with them, and that surely can't be the basis for healthy politics in our society."

BARACK OBAMA

When Obama quietly replied, "Luo," another boy hooted like a monkey, causing the whole class to break up in laughter. Before the day was out, a red-haired girl asked if she could touch his hair, and a boy asked him if his father was a cannibal.

"The novelty of having me in class quickly wore off for the other kids," Obama would later write. His fellow students, mostly the privileged children of well-off families who lived in houses far grander than the two-bedroom apartment Obama shared with his mother's parents, weren't overtly cruel. They didn't beat him up or mock him. They simply lost interest in the black kid who played soccer, badminton, and chess—games he'd learned from his Indonesian stepfather while living in Jakarta with his mother for four years before returning to Hawaii without her—but who couldn't

Obama's mother, Ann Dunham (with his Indonesian stepfather, Lolo Soetoro, and half sister Maya Soetoro), insisted that he supplement his schooling by taking U.S. correspondence courses during the four years he lived in Indonesia. Ann woke him at 4:00 a.m. every morning to instruct him for three hours before he left for school and she went to her job at the American embassy.

throw a football or ride a skateboard.

As the months passed, he managed to make a few friends and "to toss a wobbly football around," but mostly he withdrew into a routine of going home after school, reading comics, watching TV, and listening to the radio. "I felt safe," he wrote; "it was as if I had dropped into a long hibernation."

He was shocked out of it a few months after school began when his grandparents on his mother's side ("Gramps" and "Toot," short for *tutu*, the Hawaiian word for grandmother) announced that his father and namesake—who had left home to attend Harvard University in 1963 (when Obama was two years old) and had never returned—as well as his mother, Ann (who was separating from her second husband and planning to leave Jakarta and move back to Hawaii with his half sister Maya), would all be coming for the holidays.

"Should be one hell of a Christmas," Gramps said.

Years later Obama would write that while growing up, "my father remained a myth to me, both more and less than a man," a figure he knew only through the stories his mother and grandparents told and the memories, almost always fond, that they shared with him. In their stories Barack Sr. was tall and handsome, gracious and wise; he spoke in a deep baritone with a lilting British accent; he had a strong singing voice, full of personality, and he was an excellent dancer; he was both powerful and kind, honest and frank—traits that could make him seem "a bit domineering" and "uncompromising sometimes," his mother admitted. He was brilliant of mind, a Phi Beta Kappa, and charming and self-confident.

"It's a fact, Bar," Gramps said. "Your dad could handle any situation, and that made everybody like him."

In family photographs, Obama saw his father's "dark laughing face, the prominent forehead, and thick glasses that made him appear older than his years."

From his mother he learned that his father was born on the shores of Lake Victoria in a poor village where his father, Hussein Onyango Obama, was a learned elder of

their tribe, and a healer and medicine man. He taught his son to tend his herd of goats and to know the value of a good education, sending him to a local school run by the British colonial administration. Barack Sr. attended college in Nairobi on scholarship, and as Kenya prepared for independence he was chosen to go to America to continue his education so that he could return and become a leader who would help build the fledgling nation.

"His wife and his daughters come before his political career and that is crucial in a time when families are coming apart."

JEREMIAH A. WRIGHT, OBAMA'S PASTOR

In 1959 Obama's father, then twenty-three, became the first African student at the University of Hawaii. There, in a Russian-language class, Barack the elder, who, his son would write, was "black as pitch," met a cheerful, wide-eyed, eighteen-year-old freshman who was by contrast "white as milk."

Ann Dunham was the Kansas-born daughter of a furniture store manager and life insurance salesman who harbored a bohemian streak—he wrote poetry and listened to jazz—and his more pragmatic wife, the punctual employee of a local bank whose family back in Kansas could trace a branch of its lineage to a famous ancestor—Jefferson Davis, president of the Confederate States of America.

The Dunhams had moved to the islands the year after Ann's African schoolmate. The

"I've got relatives who look like Bernie Mac and I've got relatives who look like Margaret Thatcher. So we've got it all."

BARACK OBAMA

of Honolulu. His father earned his degree in economics in just three years, graduating in 1962, the year after his son was born.

Offered a generous graduate-study scholarship at the New School in New York that would have allowed him to bring his wife and son with him to the city, Obama Sr. accepted instead a tuition-only grant from Harvard, believing apparently that a Ph.D. from that world-famous institution would strengthen the portfolio he would carry with him when he returned to Kenya and took up whatever position of leadership awaited him.

Moving to Boston alone, he and Ann agreed that she and the baby would join him when his studies were complete and together they would move back to Kenya as a family.

Time and distance eroded the relationship, however, and the couple eventually divorced. Whatever memories their toddler had of his father dissolved as well.

His mother remarried and in 1967 she moved with her son and new husband, Lolo Soetoro, who was also a graduate of the University of Hawaii, to Soetoro's homeland of Indonesia.

As he grew older, Obama was told that after earning his degree at Harvard, his father had returned, alone, to Kenya, where he became an economist and an important figure in the administration of the new nation. He also remarried and had five children. Those children—four boys and a girl, Barack's mother told him—were his half brothers and sister, his family in Africa.

two began dating and after a brief courtship, wed—an act that in 1960 was a crime in most states. "In many parts of the South," Obama would write, "my father could have been strung up from a tree for merely looking at my mother the wrong way."

Newly admitted to the Union, however, Hawaii was young and relatively tolerant, and the family history includes no accounts of Obama's parents suffering abuse on the streets

A distant relative through Obama's mother's family, Confederate president Jefferson Davis (top left) would no doubt be surprised to know that the young batsman at right would grow up to run for president of the Union that Davis warred with over the issue of slavery.

His father's monthlong holiday visit to Hawaii in 1971 was painfully awkward at first, filled with long silences and disappointments. His father had recently been in a car accident and walked with a limp and a cane; he was thinner than Barack expected and he looked fragile; his eyes had a yellowy sheen, a lingering but

"He is a voice of strength and moderation, an American success story."

SEN. JOHN McCAIN ON OBAMA

unmistakable sign that he had a history of malaria. When his father ordered him to turn off the television—"He has been watching that machine constantly and now it is time for him to study!" he commanded—Barack ran to his room and slammed the door.

When his mother told him that Miss Hefty had invited his father to speak at his school, Barack panicked. He had bragged to his friends that his grandfather was a tribal chief, "like the king," and his father was the prince; he himself, he hinted, was next in line after his father to lead the Luo—a "tribe . . . of warriors," he said; the family name, Obama, he added, "means 'Burning Spear.'"

As much as he dreaded that his exaggerations would be exposed as lies, he listened enthralled along with his classmates and teachers as his father spoke vividly and eloquently about Kenya and its people and history. When he finished to much applause, a teacher told Barack "You've got a pretty impressive father."

"Your dad," said a classmate, the boy who had asked on the first day of school if his father ate people, "is pretty cool."

After that, he warmed up to his father. They attended a Dave Brubeck concert and his father gave him a basketball for Christmas. They walked around the city, and his father introduced him to old friends from college. They lay side by side on his father's bed, reading together. On the day he left, he gave Barack two records of African music that he had brought from Kenya as a present.

"Come on Barry," his father said as the record played on Gramps's stereo. "You will learn from the master."

With that his father began to sway to the music, his arms "swinging as they cast an invisible net," his head back, his eyes closed, his "hips moving in a tight circle . . . he [let] out a quick shout, bright and high."

He would remember the sound of that shout, and he would exchange letters with his father and dream about him through the years, but he would never see him again.

Soon after his father returned to Kenya, Obama left his grandparents' apartment and moved in with his mother, who was studying

After his grandfather took him to see a University of Hawaii basketball game, Obama (third from left, second row, with Punahou's junior varsity team in 1977) practiced for hours a day alone on a playground near his apartment.

for a master's in anthropology, and his half sister Maya in an apartment near his school.

He grew close to his mother during that time and it was her ideals, forged in the 1960s and stirred by the civil rights movement, that formed him. Ann drilled into him her values, Obama writes, "tolerance, equality, standing up for the disadvantaged." But when Ann urged him to return to Indonesia with her and Maya, where Ann planned to do the fieldwork necessary for her degree, he refused.

He hinted that it was because he had grown to like his school and he didn't want to be cast as the new kid again, once more the stranger, proving himself in yet another foreign world.

But the real reason, he wrote, was that he had become "engaged in a fitful interior struggle" to forge his identity, to come to grips with a basic fact of his life, that he was "a black man in America," but one with no model, no father, to learn from.

Living once again in his old bedroom in his grandparents' apartment, he settled into the universal teenage routine of school, part-time jobs, and coping with, he wrote, "turbulent desire."

Years later, when Obama was a candidate for the U.S. Senate, he told a reporter whose seventh-grade daughter had accompanied him on an interview that when he was her age, "I was such a terror that my teachers didn't know what to do with me."

And his half sister, now married and living in Honolulu, told *Time* that in high school, Barack "had powers . . . he was charismatic," said Maya Soetoro-Ng. "He had lots of friends" and such a way with women that he would go to the University of Hawaii campus to "meet university ladies."

Throughout his junior high and high school years, he studied his father's letters and tried to glean clues to the bigger mystery of who he was and who he was to become from his grandfather's circle of black friends, poker buddies, and drinking mates. But his father offered only vague aphorisms ("Like water finding its level, you will arrive at a

career that suits you," he wrote in one letter), and Gramps's pals were friendly enough, but as soon as the cards were dealt, they clammed up, leaving twelve-year-old Barry sitting at the bar of one of their hangouts in a Honolulu red-light district, "blowing bubbles into [his] drink and looking at the pornographic art on the walls."

"It was there [on the basketball court] that I would make my closest white friends, on turf where blackness couldn't be a disadvantage," Obama (going for the basket, left, and in his 1979 varsity team photo, far right, top row) wrote in *Dreams from My Father.*

From TV and radio and the movies he found some guidance, listening to Marvin Gaye croon and learning dance steps from *Soul Train*, watching the way Shaft walked

"It's that fundamental belief— I am my brother's keeper, I am my sister's keeper—that makes this country work."

BARACK OBAMA

WE GO PLAY HOOP

Thanks Tut, Gramps, Choom Gang, and Ray for all the good times.

Barry Obama

and talked, and learning the joys of humor, language, and cursing from Richard Pryor. But he also noticed how Bill Cosby never got the girl on *I Spy* and how the black guy on *Mission: Impossible* never emerged from his subterranean lair into the light of day.

If his father's letters didn't help him find his way, the Christmas present he gave his son did. Unlike football, basketball was a game he was not bad at and that he played, he wrote, "with a consuming passion that would always exceed my limited talent." In high school, he was talented enough to make the varsity team and he played pickup games at the University of Hawaii, where black players taught him some of the rules of the other, bigger game: "That respect came from what you did and not who your daddy was"; that talking trash was fine, as long as you could back it up; and that a man should never show emotions, especially hurt and fear, that he didn't want an opponent to see.

Years later he would realize, he wrote, that he "was living out a caricature of black male adolescence, itself a caricature of swaggering American manhood."

Even so, on the basketball court he found a community of friends, white and black, among the latter his closest friend, Ray—an engaging, smart, and funny athlete, an Olympic-caliber sprinter whose potbelly made him not look the part. Ray was among a growing number of black kids who had moved to Hawaii from the mainland and whose "confusion and anger," Obama

Called "Barry"—the same name his father used in America—in high school, Obama used his grandmother's nickname ("Tut," or "Toot," is short for "tutu," "grandparent" in Hawaiian) in giving props to family and friends in his 1979 senior yearbook (left). Above, the moon shines over Diamond Head at dawn.

wrote, "would help to shape my own."

Bonding between themselves, Obama and Ray and their other black friends chuckled over the ways of "white folks," enumerating the slights and insults they'd

---

"Race is still a powerful force in this country, and there are certain stereotypes I will have to deal with. But I find that when people get to know you they will judge you on your merits."

BARACK OBAMA

---

endured. For his part, Obama recalled a seventh-grader who called him a "coon," a tennis pro who told him not to touch a posted tournament match schedule because his color would rub off on it, a basketball coach who complained that opponents in a pickup game were "a bunch of niggers."

At the same time, he felt removed from the easy camaraderie of his friends. "Sometimes I would find myself talking to Ray about 'white folks' this and 'white folks' that," he wrote, "and I would suddenly remember my mother's smile, and the words that I spoke would seem awkward and false."

Though Ray often told him how much he liked Gramps and Toot, his screeds about whites and their racist deeds caused Obama to remind him that "[They] weren't living in the Jim Crow south" or a "heatless housing project in Harlem or the Bronx. We were in goddamned Hawaii!"

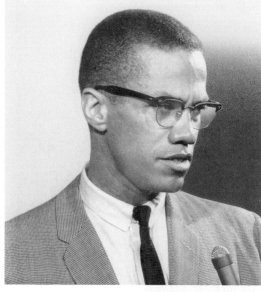

And so his life became a routine of school and basketball, hanging out with his friends, and being home in time for dinner and to help Gramps do the dishes—slipping "back and forth between my black and white worlds."

But worlds collide, in small, inexplicable ways; he would flinch when a white girl said she liked Stevie Wonder or the lady at the checkout counter asked if he played basketball or the principal told him he was a cool dude.

"His repeated acts of self-creation spoke to me," Obama wrote of Malcolm X (in a 1964 portrait, top, and speaking at a Harlem rally in 1963, above) in his memoir. "The blunt poetry of his words, his unadorned insistence on respect, promised a new and uncompromising order."

"I did like Stevie Wonder, I did love basketball, and I tried my best to be cool at all times." He tried to figure out why such seemingly innocent, offhand remarks riled him the way they did, but the answer eluded him.

In his search for role models and surrogates for the main character missing in his life, Obama found a trove in the books of James Baldwin, Ralph Ellison, Langston

Hughes, Richard Wright, and W.E.B. Du Bois. But even as he devoured them— reading not for entertainment as much as out of a hunger to discover their hidden meanings and deeply rooted truths—he was unsettled by what he found at their core. "I kept finding the same anguish," he wrote, "the same doubt; a self-contempt that neither irony nor intellect seemed able to deflect. Even Du Bois's learning and Baldwin's love and Langston's humor eventually succumbed to its corrosive force, each man finally forced to doubt art's redemptive power."

Only Malcolm X seemed not to have given up. Where the others withdrew ("exhausted, bitter men, the devil at their heels"), it seemed to Obama that Malcolm had invented his own path to redemption. But not even Malcolm could prescribe a treatment for his deepest pain, could not heal the wound of his rent worlds. "He spoke of a wish he'd once had, the wish that the white blood that ran through him, there by an act of violence"—rape—"might somehow be expunged."

For Obama, that would mean abandoning "the road to self-respect" that his search had put him on. He would be betraying himself, he wrote, if he "left my mother and my grandparents at some uncharted border."

Obama doesn't say so in his book, but during this period in his life when he was reading voraciously, educating himself, and plumbing the depths of his feelings, trying, however unsuccessfully at the time, to untangle and understand them, hoping to find the fully realized man—the father— in himself, the seed of a different kind of salvation began to germinate. He was beginning his education as a writer.

It would be decades before he would discover and realize his talent for the written word—he composed *Dreams from My Father* when he first began to practice

---

"I have a number of political heroes, including iconic figures like Dr. King, Congressman John Lewis, and President Lincoln. These leaders are visionary, they are inspiring, and they gave those of us who watched or studied them a sense of hope and purpose and a reason to get involved."

BARACK OBAMA

---

law, in the early 1990s, long before his first forays into politics. But less than two years after he graduated from high school, he would discover the writer's most essential tool and greatest gift—his voice.

"Junkie. Pothead. That's where I'd been headed: the final, fatal role of the young would-be black man."

So Obama would describe himself as an eighteen-year-old freshman at Occidental College in Los Angeles, in 1979. "Pot had helped, and booze; maybe a little blow when you could afford it. Not smack though." He didn't try heroin, he wrote, because the guy who wanted to turn him on to it was shaking and sweating, and Obama didn't like the looks of the rubber tubing he tied off with and the needle he stuck in his arm. He wanted no part of the oblivion the man was pushing; it looked too much like death.

He did drugs in those days, not because he "was trying to prove what a down brother I was," he wrote, but because the high helped him "push questions of who I was out of my mind."

Occidental's was an idyllic, leafy campus, near Pasadena and far from the sprawling ghettos on the south side of L.A. Obama

meeting. "I'm not black," she said. "I'm multiracial!"

Scornful as he was of those students' self-denial, he recognized part of himself in their "mixed-up hearts . . . Their confusion made me question my own racial credentials all over again."

"If you feel good about me, there's a whole lot of young men out there who could be me if given the chance."

BARACK OBAMA

was easily accepted into the black student population, many of them kids from the ghettos who were happy to have escaped the gritty and dangerous streets they'd grown up on. "I hadn't grown up in Compton, or Watts," Obama wrote. "I had nothing to escape from except my own inner doubt."

Then there were the black kids from the suburbs, like one beautiful coed who got offended when Obama asked her if she was going to a Black Students' Association

While Obama spent much of his time on Punahou's playfields (above) and received only "marginal report cards," he wrote, he devoured books by James Baldwin, Langston Hughes, Richard Wright, and other favorites that he found on the shelves of the school's library, located inside Cooke Hall (right).

"I am not opposed to all wars. I'm opposed to dumb wars."

BARACK OBAMA

Aligning himself with students whose black cred was unassailable, he made friends with one righteous dorm mate whose sister had been a founding member of a midwest Black Panther Party chapter and who himself had had run-ins with the police and had friends in jail. "His lineage was pure, his loyalties clear, and for that reason he always made me feel a little off-balance."

KUSUNOKI *first row:* Eric Kusunoki, Amy Boardman, Brian Wright, Sarah Brown, Janet Sprenger, Be *second row:* Julie Cooke, Tim Robinson, Kam Chun, Vernette Ferreira, Billy Stoner, Whitey Kahooha Nobunaga, Ira Lim, Dean Ando, Robin Helbling, Janet Totaro, Jill Okihiro, Matt Martinson

The strategy, to show that he was just as righteous as his dorm mate, backfired when, to Obama's lingering shame, he mocked another friend, a black student, but one from a middle-class background who dressed like a preppy, "talked like Beaver Cleaver" and had a white girlfriend, for being a bogus brother.

"Why you say that, man?" said his dorm

oldberg, Pam Schuler, Julie Kim,
o, Byron Ho, Barry Obama, Brian

Looking dapper in Mr. Eric Kusunoki's Punahou homeroom, Obama (left, standing center) first tested his writing talents on the staff of the school's literary journal, *Ka Wai Ola* ("The Living Water"). He posed (above) with his schoolmates for the yearbook in his senior year (second row, right).

mate. "Seems to me we should be worrying about whether our own stuff's together instead of passing judgment on how other folks are supposed to act."

Later, the memory of that incident and the shame it induced, helped snap him out of his pot haze. It was his own fear of not belonging, he realized, that led him to ridicule his friend—the fear "that unless I dodged and hid and pretended to be something I wasn't I would forever remain an outsider, with the rest of the world, black and white, always standing in judgment."

He understood finally that he did not have to be slave to fear and anger and despair, that both worlds, black and white—his father's and mother's—were part of him and "only a lack of imagination, a failure of nerve," he wrote, "had made me think that I had to choose" between them.

"Policy-by-slogan will no longer pass as an acceptable form of debate in this country."

BARACK OBAMA

A glimpse into the future occurred during his sophomore year, his last at Occidental, when, with the encouragement of a girlfriend, he became involved in the nationwide student movement to demand that colleges and universities divest themselves of financial interests that helped support the apartheid government of South Africa.

At a student rally, Obama rose to speak in public for the first time.

"There's a struggle going on," he said as students playing Frisbee on the campus common turned to listen along with a throng of students and professors. "It's happening an ocean away. But it's a struggle that touches each and every one of us . . . a struggle that demands we choose sides. Not between black and white. Not between rich and poor. No . . .

It's a choice between dignity and servitude. Between fairness and injustice. Between commitment and indifference. A choice between right and wrong."

"Go on with it, Barack! Tell it like it is!" someone shouted.

But by prearrangement, he was dragged off stage by two students dressed as soldiers,

as an agitprop bit to dramatize the lack of free-speech rights in South Africa. As his friends pulled him away, however, he didn't want to give up the microphone. The audience was "clapping and cheering, and I knew that I had them, that the connection had been made . . . I really wanted to stay up there, to hear my voice bouncing off the crowd and returning back to me in applause. I had so much left to say."

Pauahi Hall is the centerpiece of Punahou's lush campus. During his years there—and later at Occidental College—Obama wrestled, he wrote, "in a fitful interior struggle" to find his identity as a man in the two vividly drawn—and fatherless— black and white worlds he was growing up in.

FINDING HIS WAY

During his time at Columbia University (right and top), where Obama transferred for his junior and senior years, he lived on a since-gentrified block on New York City's East Ninety-fourth Street (above). He was living there when he learned in a 1982 phone call from an aunt in Africa that his father had died in an auto accident.

3

I hope you don't feel resentful toward him," Barack Obama's mother said when he asked her if she had an overseas stamp for a letter he had written to his father.

He said, "No," but more than a decade had passed since he'd last seen him, and their correspondence had slowed to a trickle. He felt so estranged from his father in fact that he had started an earlier draft of the letter by writing "Dear Dr. Obama."

It was the summer between his junior and senior years at Columbia University and his mother and half sister Maya had come to visit him in New York, where he was working on a construction site and living in an apartment uptown at the edge of East Harlem that he shared with a Pakistani friend he'd known in Los Angeles.

He had transferred to Columbia determined to break out of the cocoon Occidental provided and the bad habits and self-indulgences he had found himself susceptible to there; at the same time he was eager to escape L.A.'s suburban sprawl and live "in the heart of a true city," with black neighborhoods in close proximity.

Obama arrived in New York at the glitzy dawn of the go-go 1980s, when Wall

Street was booming and "Manhattan was humming" with new and more-expensive restaurants and nightclubs opening what seemed like nightly to cater to an exploding population of young urban professionals, "men and women barely out of their twenties [and] already enjoying ridiculous wealth."

Feeling the need to steel himself from temptation, Obama concentrated on his studies and resisted the invitation of his jovial, bar- and girl-crawling roommate's nightly forays. "You're becoming a bore," his roommate said, and Obama, who ran three miles a day, fasted on Sundays and began keeping a journal in earnest (writing what he called "daily reflections and very bad poetry" but also passages that would become the source material for the memoir he would write a decade later), could not deny it was true.

When he wasn't attending classes or studying, he explored the city on foot and saw "beneath the hum" of the dazzling city the legions of unemployed and the abandoned, rat- and crack-infested tenements where the homeless took refuge and drug dealers preyed upon them. Little of the Reagan administration's touted "trickle down" economy seemed to be seeping far enough to thaw the permafreeze of poverty that trapped the have-nots in an underclass from which there seemed to be no escape.

"It was as if the middle ground had collapsed, utterly," he wrote, leaving rich and poor on opposite sides of the ever-widening maw between them. It was a racial as well as an economic gulf that threatened to become a cauldron, seething with hatred. Not even the hallowed halls of academia were immune from "the bile that flowed freely not just out on the streets but in the stalls of Columbia's bathrooms as well, where, no matter how many times the administration tried to paint them over, the walls remained scratched with blunt correspondence between niggers and kikes."

When his mother and sister visited in the summer of 1982, they found a young man far different from the disaffected slacker they would have encountered had they dropped by his dorm at Occidental three years before.

His mother was especially pleased to learn that he was writing to let his father know that he planned to visit Kenya after graduation the following summer. "I think it'll be wonderful for you two to finally get to know each other," she said and then went on to share her memories of his father, including one story about how he was an hour late for their first date. Waiting for him outside the university library, she'd fallen asleep on a bench. She woke to find her future husband standing over her with two friends. "You see, gentlemen," he said. "I told you that she was a fine girl, and that she would wait for me."

The way she told the story, smiling and laughing as she spoke, he saw the depth of her enduring love for his father. Even though he'd left her with a baby to raise on her own and she'd divorced him as a result, she loved him still. "She saw my father as everyone hopes at least one other person might see them," Obama wrote, adding that she had tried to make him, "the child who never knew him, see him in the same way."

Any hope of that happening appeared to end for good just a few months later when he received a telephone call from an aunt in Nairobi. His father had been killed in a car crash. He was forty-six years old. His son didn't shed a tear.

While his fellow Columbia graduates applied for high-paying corporate jobs or sent their applications off to grad schools, Obama felt fired by a passion instilled in him by stirring stories his mother told him as a boy about the civil rights movement and its brave freedom riders and heroic martyrs, and stirred as well by his own idealistic desire to give back to the community and to do what he could to help the powerless and disenfranchised free themselves from the cycle of poverty and despair he saw all around.

Instead of mapping a path for a rapid ascent up the money ladder, he prepared for his graduation from Columbia in 1983 by writing letters to dozens of civil rights organizations, progressive politicians like Chicago's recently elected Harold Washington (the city's first black mayor), tenants' rights groups, and neighborhood associations all across the country.

When he heard back from a grand total of no one, he decided to bide his time, find a job, pay off his college loans, and try again. This time his job search was almost too successful. Hired by the multinational Business International Corporation as a research assistant, he was soon promoted to a higher-paying position as financial writer, with his own office, his own secretary, and money to burn, not to mention the admiration of the black women in the secretarial pool who took pride in him and predicted that one day he'd be running the company.

Obama was beginning to think he might like doing just that when he received another phone call from Africa, reminding him who he was. It was his half sister Auma calling to report another accident, another death. Another of his father's children—a boy named David, his half brother—had been killed in a motorcycle accident.

He wasn't sure why, but the news of the death of a stranger an ocean away who was also a brother reminded him that he had made a commitment to serve—or at least to become involved in something more important than an office on a higher floor with a better view. A few months later, he turned in his resignation and sent out another batch of letters looking for a job as a community organizer.

"There's nothing wrong with making money, but focusing your life solely on making a buck shows a poverty of ambition."

BARACK OBAMA

After six months, he got an offer to work as a trainee with a veteran grassroots organizer who was working to start job placement and training centers in neighborhoods on the South Side of Chicago that had been hard hit by plant closings and layoffs. The pay, $10,000 a year, with a $2,000 allowance to buy a car, would have been scoffed at by his friends—even the security guard in his office building told him, "Forget about this organizing business and do something that's gonna make you some money . . . you can't help folks that ain't gonna make it no how, and they won't appreciate you trying"—but he took the job anyway.

Obama fell in love with Chicago as soon as he drove around it—cruising the shoreline drive along Lake Michigan and through the heart of the city the length of Martin Luther King Drive; he found the Regal Theater where Duke Ellington and Ella Fitzgerald used to perform, and as he went he recalled reading about Richard Wright delivering mail in

"Our individual salvation depends on collective salvation."

BARACK OBAMA

Chicago while awaiting the publication of his first book. Obama communed with the ghosts of the multitudes—those who made the great migration north from the Delta, seeking a better life and bringing their joyous and mournful, soul-stirring blues with them.

On his third day in town he happened into Smitty's Barbershop, a neighborhood place where the almost mythic warmth and easy conviviality made Obama feel instantly at home. He was just leaving when Smitty, the barber, told him he ought to "come back a little sooner next time. Your hair was looking awful raggedy when you walked in." Obama, who now lives with his wife and kids in nearby Hyde Park, has been coming back ever since.

If, however unintentionally, the intensive reading, journal-writing, and self-analysis Obama engaged in as a student provided the first foundations for his future career as a writer, the three years he spent in Chicago as a community organizer served as his political apprenticeship. And a demanding challenge it was, one fraught with frustration and infrequent rewards but one that taught him firsthand the plight of America's inner cities and the resilience of residents who feel at once powerless and hopeful that things can change.

Working with a tiny network of community activists and volunteers from South Side churches who were attempting to help residents improve conditions— and, often, simply cope—in deteriorating neighborhoods plagued by sky-high unemployment, crime, and high school dropout and teen-pregnancy rates; where city services,

Obama still lends a hand in the Chicago neighborhoods where he worked as a community organizer in the 1980s. Here he and Catherine Moore, a worker at the St. James Food Pantry, hand out Thanksgiving groceries in 2006.

including police protection, were slow or faulty at best, where parks were left untended and schools underfunded, where stores were closed and boarded up and where sometimes it seemed only those who couldn't afford to leave stayed, Obama did the same thing he would do when he later ran for office: he knocked on doors, attended neighborhood meetings in church basements, school cafeterias, housing projects, lunch counters, barbershops, and street corners.

Three decades later, in January 2007 when he announced his intentions to run for the presidency, Obama alluded to his years as a community organizer in Chicago when he said in a video statement to supporters, "I learned that meaningful change always begins at the grassroots, and that engaged citizens working together can accomplish extraordinary things."

"You can't always come up with the optimal solution, but you can usually come up with a better solution."

BARACK OBAMA

Back in the mid-1980s, as he canvassed the neighborhoods of Chicago's South Side, he listened as people told him of their hardships and hopes and their anger. He and his group helped when they could, but often failed. When a woman he spoke with told him that a friend of her son's had been shot at in the street in front of his house, Obama met with other parents worried about increasing gang violence in their neighborhood and organized a meeting with a police district

commander, only to have the officer cancel and send in his place a department public relations rep who lectured the parents on the need to discipline their children.

He had better luck with campaigns he spearheaded to get schools to adopt a counseling and mentoring program for at-risk teenagers and to organize residents of South Side housing projects to demand that the city fulfill its asbestos-removal and job-training promises in the projects as effectively as in other better-connected wards. Small neighborhood groups organized by Obama and his colleagues operated street cleanup campaigns and Crime Watch programs, successfully sought improved sanitation service from the city, and got the parks department to clean up and improve South Side green spaces and playgrounds.

His successes brought him some attention around town; he was invited to speak and join panels. "Local politicians knew my name," he wrote, "even if they still couldn't pronounce it."

Even so, the city's problems often seemed overwhelming and after three frequently frustrating years in Chicago, Obama realized he was tilting against the Windy City's entrenched, immovable power structure; as a street corner–church basement organizer he could work for twenty years and continue to run up against the same impediments— red tape, corruption, neighborhood leaders more interested in protecting their turf than improving it, and indifference. To effect real change, he needed clout, the kind wielded by the lawyers and politicians who held the real power in the city. And so he applied to law school, "to learn power's currency in all its intricacy and detail," he wrote.

Before he left Chicago, promising

It was at Chicago's Trinity United Church of Christ where Obama (attending a service there in 2004) heard the phrase "the audacity of hope" in a sermon delivered by his pastor, Rev. Jeremiah Wright Jr., on his first visit to the church two decades ago.

to return after earning his law degree at Harvard, he attended a rousing service at the South Side's Trinity United Church of Christ, where the full-throated congregation sang along with the gospel choir, their voices buoyed by organ surges as they swayed to a drummer's backbeat.

The sermon that Sunday, punctuated by shouts of "Say it!" and "Yessuh!" from the congregation, spoke to the myriad hardships—from overdue electric bills to marital abuse and failed schools—endured by those gathered there. The preacher identified the enemy common to all—despair—and its antidote, one without which no Freedom Rides would ever have been attempted, without which no artist would ever pick up a pen, no people would ever strive to create a better world. The sermon was called "The Audacity of Hope."

Obama never forgot it.

By the time he arrived in Kenya in 1987 for a monthlong visit prior to moving to Boston to begin law school, he had already learned some surprising truths about his father from his half sister Auma. During an earlier visit to Chicago, she had told Obama that she and her brother Roy were born before their father left for Hawaii in 1959 and were living with their mother in Kogelo when he returned from America with a new wife, a white woman named Ruth. Auma and Roy went to live in Nairobi with their father—who was working for an American oil company—and Ruth, who eventually bore him two more children.

"The Old Man," as his African children called Obama's father, owned a large house in Nairobi, drove a big car, and enjoyed high status and privileges thanks to friends in the highest reaches of the new government of independent Kenya. After he quit the oil company and joined the government, working in the Ministry of Tourism, however, he had a falling out with the president, Jomo Kenyatta, after

tensions grew between Kenyatta's tribe—the Kikuyus, the largest in Kenya—and the Old Man's Luos.

Before long the Old Man was fired from his post and blacklisted; finding doors in all the ministries and government agencies closed to him, he ended up with an insignificant job in the Water Department.

Despondent over his reduced status and angry that his old friends treated him like a pariah, he began drinking heavily and frequently lost his temper with his wife and children. Ruth left him while he was recovering in the hospital for nearly a

Obama learned the true story of his father's life from his step-grandmother (right) during his first visit to Kenya in 1987. Political differences with the nation's first president, Jomo Kenyatta, led Obama's father, Barack (left), to years of poverty and despair. Obama's older half brother Malik (below, in 2004), who lives in eastern Kenya, holds a photo of himself with his famous American brother and an unidentified friend.

"What I want to be able to do if possible, and it's not always possible, is to engage people who disagree with me in a dialogue."

BARACK OBAMA

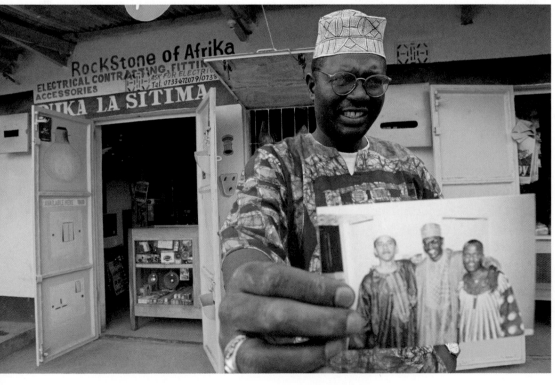

year after a car accident in which the other driver, a white farmer, had been killed. (It was after he was released from the hospital that Obama's father visited Hawaii, to spend Christmas with his then-ten-year-old son.)

Upon his return, he lost his job at the Water Department and had to move with his children into a dilapidated house in the slums of Nairobi.

By the time of his death, things had improved somewhat. He had returned to government following Kenyatta's death, working in the Ministry of Finance, and had even fathered another son. Yet despite flashes of his old charm, his last years, Auma said, were tinged with bitterness and regret.

It's only when you hitch yourself up to something bigger than yourself that you realize your true potential."

BARACK OBAMA

For Obama, hearing this utterly unexpected accounting of his father's life, one that trampled all the myths that his mother and grandparents had woven for him, was unsettling to say the least. "I felt as if my world had been turned on its head; as if I had woken up to find a blue sun in the yellow sky; or heard animals speaking like men."

When he met Dorsila, the youngest child of his great-great-grandfather Obama, who was in turn the great-great-great-great grandson of Owiny, the legendary Luo warrior whose

armies defeated the Bantu nine generations before the white man came to Kisumu, she was startled when he pulled out a Bic to light his cigarette.

"She wants to know where the fire comes from," Auma explained. "She says that things are changing so fast it makes her head spin. She says that the first time she saw television, she [thought] the people inside the box . . . were very rude, because when she spoke to them they never answered back."

They were all sitting under a mango tree outside the house his father had built for his grandmother, one story, with crumbling concrete walls and a corrugated-tin roof, bougainvillea abloom all around, chickens pecking at the bare ground.

On a wall inside the house in Kogelo, a village about fifty miles north of the equator and near the shore of Lake Victoria —where just a few generations previously the clan existed as their people had for hundreds of years, living in a family compound, wearing nothing but goatskin loincloths, raising goats, and planting corn —hung his father's doctorate diploma from Harvard University.

Dorsila, who spoke only Luo, listened in nonetheless as Obama and Auma's "Granny," the same step-grandmother, now in her late eighties, whom Senator Obama and his wife and children met with in the summer of 2006, shared the oral history of their family.

"First there was Miwiru. It's not known who came before. Miwiru sired Sigoma, Sigoma sired Owiny . . ." She spoke in the cadence of Genesis, eventually tracing Mirwiru's descendants forward thirteen generations to the future United States Senator Obama. "When your grandfather was still a boy," she said, "we began to hear that the white man had come to Kisumu town. It was said that these white men had skin as soft as a child's, but that they rode on a ship that roared like thunder and had sticks that burst with fire."

Obama listened spellbound, much as his ancestors had when they gathered around the fire to listen to the wise elders or to itinerant harpist-poets as they "sang of great deeds of the past."

But Granny's oral history was not of heroic deeds but of the wrenching change brought by the British, whose rule by gun and tax collector destroyed the Luo's ancient way of life in the span of a single generation. Obama's grandfather was among the first of his clan to adopt the white man's ways—trading his loincloth for suits and shoes, learning to speak, read, and write English—only to wind up embittered and broken after a lifetime of servitude to his colonial masters.

From Granny, Obama learned that the father who had abandoned him had been himself abandoned, at age nine, by his mother, and as a teenager beaten bloody and banished from home by his father for his rebellious spirit. Despite his stellar grades, he was expelled from a mission school—"He would sneak girls into his dormitory," Granny said, "for he could always talk very sweetly to girls"—and when he was arrested and jailed for his involvement in the independence movement, his father refused to bail him out. Obama learned from his grandmother how his father was released soon after, but by twenty his dreams and ambitions to get the education he needed to create a better life had disappeared. He was married, with a son and a daughter—Auma—on the way,

working at a menial job in Nairobi, and had no hope of ever achieving the bright future in an independent Kenya that he'd always imagined. Instead he would remain mired in poverty, stooped like his own father by despair and bitterness.

But then a chance meeting with two American educators living in Nairobi changed his life. They befriended him and, impressed by his bright mind and engaging manner, promised to help him get into a university if he completed a correspondence course for a secondary degree. Obama's father did as they suggested, passed the course, and proceeded to write dozens of letters to colleges and universities in America.

When Granny finished her story, she showed Obama copies of more than thirty letters, each with recommendations from his two American friends, that his father had written to schools in the United States and sent overseas.

Those letters were "like messages in a bottle," Obama thought later in reverie as he stood beside his father's unmarked grave at the rear of his grandmother's compound in Kogelo. "How lucky he must have felt when his ship came sailing in! He must have known, when that [acceptance] letter came from Hawaii, that he had been chosen after all; that he possessed the grace of his name, the *baraka*, the blessing of God."

As he stood there beside the grave, he felt that he knew and understood—and forgave—his father for the first time in his life. His father had not succumbed to despair. He had had the audacity to hope.

And for the first time, his son wept for him.

POLITICAL APPRENTICESHIP

In the summer after his first year at Harvard Law School (above), Obama (receiving his diploma in 1991, right), began dating Michelle Robinson, an attorney in the Chicago corporate law office where he interned. His mother, Ann, who posed with Michelle's mom, Marian, at the couple's 1992 wedding (far right), died three years later of cancer. *The Audacity of Hope* is dedicated to Obama's mother, "whose loving spirit sustains me still."

"Get in line. Please don't grab. Folks, you're going to have to be patient."

MAN SELLING OBAMA T-SHIRTS AND BUTTONS

OUTSIDE A SEATTLE RALLY

Waiting in the wings at the Fleet Center in Boston, where he was to give the keynote address at the 2004 Democratic Convention, Barack Obama had good reason to be nervous. And not just because he had been allotted seventeen minutes of uninterrupted prime time on all three broadcast networks and cable and satellite feeds that would carry his speech around the world.

An utterly obscure Illinois state senator who had met John Kerry, his party's presidential standard-bearer, for the first time during the Illinois primary earlier that year when he spoke at a Kerry fundraiser, Obama was surprised and flattered a few weeks later when he received word that Kerry wanted him to speak at the convention. When Kerry's campaign manager called before the convention to tell Obama that he would be speaking not merely to state caucuses or to introduce one of the party's big guns to the delegates but delivering the keynote address, he was shocked.

And so was just about everyone else.

Democrats well remembered that in 1988, when another obscure politician

"We have an Administration that believes that the government's role is to protect the powerful from the powerless," Obama said (addressing the Democratic Convention, left, and campaigning for the Senate in Chicago in 2004, right and below).

named Bill Clinton was tapped to deliver the keynote, the speech at the convention didn't go over any better than the party's candidate Michael Dukakis would in the general election that year.

Among the party faithful gathered at the Fleet Center, more than a few delegates surely were disappointed that some nobody from the midwest was going to address them rather than the likes of the Roosevelts and Kennedys of the party's glory years or, yes, Clinton, whose silver tongue had eventually carried them back into power four years after the Dukakis debacle.

Even David Axelrod, Obama's longtime friend and campaign manager, was "a nervous wreck" as zero hour approached. Obama tried to reassure him as the two arrived at the convention center. "I remember him patting me on the shoulder and saying 'Don't worry about it,'" Axelrod later recalled. "'I'll make my marks.'"

But alone in the green room with his wife, Michelle, an attorney who mentored him when he worked in the summer of 1988 at her firm after his first year in law school, he admitted he was feeling a bit queasy.

Obama recounts the moment in *The Audacity of Hope*: "She hugged me tight, looked into my eyes and said—'Just don't screw it up, buddy!'"

He didn't.

Wearing a borrowed tie, he stood on the dais and delivered a speech that Democrats—and many Republicans—hail as one

"I'm a Democrat because we are the party that believes we're all in this together."

BARACK OBAMA

"Our party has chosen a man to lead us who embodies the best this country has to offer." Obama (top, and with Michelle, above) was talking about John Kerry at the 2004 Democratic Convention. He hopes the same will be said of him in 2008.

of the greatest political convention keynotes in memory.

The convention hall rang with cheers as Obama spoke of the "true genius of America," a nation where "we can say what we think, write what we think, without hearing a sudden knock on the door . . . [where] we can participate in the political process without fear of retribution, and [know] that our votes will be counted—or at least, most of the time."

When he said that we live in a dangerous world where "war must be an option, but it should never be the first option," there was no mistaking what he was talking about. He spoke about a young Marine bound for Iraq and eager to serve and perhaps die for his country. "I thought this young man was all any of us might hope for in a child. But then I asked myself: Are we serving [him] as well as he was serving us?"

And he stirred raw emotions when he spoke about the war's toll of soldiers killed—

it was 900 then, more than 2,000 deaths ago—and maimed, returning home "with a limb missing or with nerves shattered."

A no-man-is-an-island theme ran through the speech: "If there's a child on the South Side of Chicago who can't read, that matters to me . . . If there's a senior citizen somewhere who can't pay for her prescription and has to choose between medicine and the rent, that makes my life poorer . . . If there's an Arab American family being rounded up without benefit of an attorney or due process, that threatens my civil liberties."

But it was his call for all citizens to come together in "a united American family" that many found most memorable: "[T]here's not a liberal America and a conservative America . . . There's not a black America and white America . . . there's the United States of America.

"The pundits like to slice-and-dice our country into Red States and Blue States . . . But I've got news for them . . . We worship an awesome God in the Blue States, and we don't like federal agents poking around our libraries in the Red States. We coach Little League in the Blue States and have gay friends in the Red States."

Closing with a plea that "out of this long political darkness a bright day will come," the speech was greeted by thunderous applause and ecstatic reviews for Obama's "mesmerizing" and "phenomenal" performance. *Time* rated it "one of the best speeches in convention history," and even the conservative *National Review* said the "simple and powerful" address was deserving of the "rapturous critical reception" it received.

In the aftermath of the torrent of praise and publicity, Obama would coast to victory in his own race for the U.S. Senate and score one of the few triumphs Democrats could cheer in an election in which they could not win the presidency and lost seats in both houses of Congress.

And so America's brightest new political star was born.

"Barack is the American dream . . . he is absolutely the best this country has to offer—and that makes the Democratic Party proud."

TERRY McAULIFFE, FORMER CHAIRMAN, DEMOCRATIC NATIONAL COMMITTEE

Wowing with his performance was nothing new for Obama, who first made national news in 1990 when he became the first black student elected president of Harvard Law School's prestigious *Law Review.* The resulting publicity brought calls from editors in New York who encouraged him to begin work on his memoirs, a heady proposition for a grad student not yet thirty years old.

His fellow students were impressed by his grace in the spotlight. "He didn't carry himself like the big man on campus that he clearly was," said Hill Harper, a former Harvard classmate-turned-actor (*CSI: New York*). And his constitutional law professor, Laurence Tribe—who would argue Al Gore's case against George W. Bush before the Supreme Court during the disputed election of 2000—chose him as his research assistant and later called Obama "one of the two most talented students I've had in thirty-seven years in teaching." (We're still waiting to learn the name of the other).

"After Harvard, Obama could have done anything he wanted," said David Axelrod. "He could have gone to the most opulent of law firms." Or, better yet for a graduating

"Ultimately I trust the judgment of the American people. . . . If I ever did decide to run, I'm confident that I'd be run through the paces pretty good."

BARACK OBAMA

law student with lofty ambitions, a clerkship on the U.S. Court of Appeals, considered the fast track to clerking on the Supreme Court. But when appeals court Chief Justice Abner Mikva tried to hire him as his clerk, Obama said no thanks.

Before he graduated magna cum laude in 1991 Obama was being recruited by Wall Street firms and large corporate partnerships from across the country. When Chicago civil rights attorney Judd Miner read what turned out to be an erroneous report that Obama planned to join a silk-stocking firm in Chicago, he put in a call to the *Law Review*. The secretary who answered told him Obama wasn't in and asked if this was a recruiting call.

"I said 'I guess so,'" Miner recounted years later. "She said 'I'll put you on the list, you're number 643' or something like that."

Obama turned down the higher-paying jobs and to the delight of Miner and his partners took the position at the firm of Miner, Barnhill & Galland, where he worked on discrimination cases. "There aren't many blindingly talented people, and most of them are pains in the ass," one of the partners told *Time* after Obama left to run for the U.S. Senate. But "Barack," he added, "is the whole package."

Between cases, Obama worked on his memoir and in 1992, headed a statewide voter registration drive called Project VOTE that added 150,000 voters to the rolls and was credited with helping Bill Clinton carry Illinois in that year's election.

He also found time to teach constitutional law as a senior lecturer at the University of Chicago Law School, which he continued through January 2004, a full year after he began his race for the U.S. Senate. "Teaching keeps you sharp," Obama told the *New Yorker* that year. "The great thing about teaching constitutional law is that all the tough questions land in your lap: abortion, gay rights, affirmative action. And you need to be able to argue both sides.

I have to be able to argue the other side as well as [conservative Supreme Court Judge Antonin] Scalia does. I think that's good for one's politics."

When Obama decided to try his hand at making law in addition to teaching it, he set his sights on an open Illinois state senate seat in a district that included both the university neighborhood of Hyde Park where he lived and some of the poorest neighborhoods in Chicago. Before launching his campaign however, he had to clear it with his wife, Michelle, herself a no-nonsense lawyer who looked dimly on politics.

"I said, 'I married you because you're cute and you're smart, but this is the

"He's not a guy who's looking to people to tell him what to do," aide David Axelrod said of Obama (keeping his own counsel during an interview, left and above; and working in his Senate office in 2004, right). "He knows who he is and what he wants to do."

dumbest thing you could have ever asked me to do,'" she later said in an interview. "Fortunately for all of us, Barack wasn't as cynical as I was."

Tall, bright, and gorgeous, Michelle, born in 1964, grew up half a continent and an ocean away from the homes in Indonesia and Honolulu where Obama grew up. "He had this mixed-up, international childhood, while I was Chicago all the way," Michelle, from a large family in a mostly black, blue-collar neighborhood on the South Side, told the *New Yorker* in 2004. "My grandmother lived five blocks away. Ozzie and Harriet, Barack called it," she said.

"I was just a typical South Side little black girl," she said. And one whose grades in school were good enough to get into Princeton University, where her older brother, Craig, was a star on the basketball team. "Of course it was different, being black," she told the *New Yorker*. "It was also different not being filthy rich."

After graduating cum laude from Princeton, Michelle also went to Harvard Law but didn't meet Obama until he arrived as a summer associate at the large

"This is a new low in American politics," a newsman said of the aggressive tactics of Justin Warfel (with Obama, right), a Republican operative hired to videotape Obama's every move during the 2004 Senate race. His opponent apologized, and Obama (waiting to speak at an Illinois church later that year, above) continued his campaign unmolested.

corporate law firm where she worked in Chicago. Sharing Obama's discomfort in the boardrooms of high-end firms, she eventually left to start up a nonprofit leadership development program before going to work for the University of Chicago Hospitals, where she is now vice president for community relations.

They were married at the Trinity United Church of Christ, which they have attended ever since, in 1992 by Rev. Jeremiah A. Wright, the Chicago preacher whose "Audacity of Hope" sermon had so impressed Obama. Her family and most of his, including his mother and half sisters Maya and Auma, attended the ceremony. "Our families get along great," Michelle told the *New Yorker*. After all, she pointed out, "we're both midwesterners. Underneath it all, he's very Kansas, because of his grandparents and his mom."

In 1996, after securing the support of his somewhat skeptical wife and encouragement from friends, colleagues at the university, and contacts he'd made as a civil rights lawyer, Obama, then thirty-five, ran for the Illinois legislature in the same South Side district where he had worked as a community activist and organizer a decade earlier. "I entered the race and proceeded to do what every first-time candidate does: I talked to anyone who would listen," he recalled in *The Audacity of Hope*. "I went to block club meetings and church socials, beauty shops and barbershops. If two guys were standing on a corner, I would cross the street to hand them campaign literature."

The tactics hadn't changed much since another Illinois lawyer, Abe Lincoln, first campaigned for office, and they paid off for Obama, who won the race and arrived for the 1997 legislative session in Springfield, the state capital where Lincoln launched his political career and where Obama would formally announce his own presidential bid ten years later.

Like Washington in 2005, Springfield in 1996 had a minority Democrat assembly presided over by a Republican chief executive. "Democrats in Springfield," Obama wrote, "would shout and holler and fulminate, and then stand by helplessly as Republicans passed large corporate tax breaks, stuck it to labor, or slashed social services."

"Take a leap of faith with me."

BARACK OBAMA

In a revealing scene in his book, Obama recalls a debate in which a Republican senator "worked himself into a lather" over a proposal to provide breakfasts to preschoolers because "it would crush their spirit of self-reliance.

"I had to point out," Obama writes, "that not too many five-year-olds I knew were self-reliant, but children who spent their formative years too hungry to learn could very well end up being charges of the state." The bill was defeated initially (a modified version later passed) and "Illinois preschoolers," he writes, "were temporarily saved from the debilitating effects of cereal and milk."

But needling opponents wasn't Obama's style when he joined the senate. Instead he worked with colleagues on both sides of the aisle, forged friendships over beers

"When people told me I couldn't win a Senate race in Illinois," said Obama (meeting with campaign aides, center; hands-free phoning in a hotel room, below right; and speaking at his Senate victory party, left, with Michelle and his daughters), "I didn't believe them."

"I think what people are most hungry for in politics right now is authenticity."

BARACK OBAMA

and bipartisan poker games—"I'm putting his kids through college," moaned one poker-playing Democrat—and won over just about everyone. "When he first came to Springfield, many resented his good looks, his articulate speaking ability, and his intellect," Republican state senator Kirk Dillard told *Washingtonian* magazine. But Obama impressed with his work ethic and commitment to getting things done. "He'll show up at any meeting that requires his attention," said Dillard. "If Barack has any enemies out there, they come from just sheer jealousy. I don't believe he has any enemies who have a good reason."

"I knew from the day he walked into this chamber that he was destined for great things," another GOP senator told the *New Yorker*. "He's to the left of me on gun control, abortion. But he can really work with Republicans."

While not all his initiatives flew—one that he proposed in his first term to

"If you are a personal investment banker, you certainly want to invest in the Barack Obama IPO. . . . It is a solid investment in the American political scene."

SEN. DICK DURBIN

amend the state constitution to include health care as a right of all Illinois residents got nowhere—he successfully amended Republican tax-cut bills to include relief for low-income families. He skillfully worked a campaign-finance reform bill through the senate and got bills passed to expand early-childhood education programs and stop usurious lenders from charging sky-high mortgage rates to low-income would-be homeowners. "It's remarkable that a reform-minded newcomer could get as much accomplished as he did," Abner Mikva, the federal Court of Appeals judge who once tried to hire Obama, told *Washingtonian.* "He made a lot of friends."

During the first six of his eight years in the senate that he was in the minority party, Obama told *Harper's*, "I passed maybe ten bills . . . Most [were] in partnership with Republicans. The first year we were in the majority . . . I passed twenty-six bills in one year."

Many of those came out of the Health and Human Services Committee, which he chaired once the Democrats won control of the senate. But Obama's most innovative, controversial, and politically impressive success was his landmark 2003 bill to require police in Illinois to videotape interrogations in all capital crime cases.

Though convinced that capital punishment does not work as a deterrent, he does believe, he writes, that "there are some crimes—mass murder, the rape and murder of a child—so heinous, so beyond the pale, that the community is justified in expressing the full measure of its outrage by meting out the ultimate punishment."

At the same time, capital cases in Illinois at the time "were so rife with error, questionable police tactics, racial bias and shoddy lawyering" that thirteen wrongly convicted death row prisoners were exonerated and the governor, a Republican, was forced to order a moratorium on executions.

Despite the obvious need for reform, Obama began with virtually no support for his proposal—police and prosecutors were opposed, as were the newly elected Democratic governor and senators in both parties who feared being tagged soft on crime; even anti-death penalty groups were wary of reform rather than outright abolition.

Over a period of weeks, Obama convened meetings of all those groups who initially opposed the legislation; rather than arguing the morality of the death penalty, Obama got everyone to agree on "the basic principle that no innocent person should end up on death row, and that no person guilty of a capital offense should go free." In the meetings Obama convinced police and prosecutors that videotaped interrogations would be a "powerful tool to convict the guilty," he later told *Time*, as well as save the innocent. While Obama and his supporters agreed to modify the bill when police said parts of it would hinder investigations, he refused their proposal that they videotape only confessions and not the entire interrogation because, he wrote, "the whole purpose of the bill was to give the public confidence that confessions were obtained free of coercion." In the end, the bill was passed unanimously and became law.

"A good compromise, a good piece of legislation, is like a good sentence. Or a good piece of music," Obama told the *New Yorker* the following year. "Everybody can recognize it. They say 'Huh. It works. It makes sense.' That doesn't happen too often [in politics], of course, but it happens."

After the thumping he received in 2000 when he lost the primary for Bobby Rush's congressional seat by a two-to-one margin, a Chicago pundit asked on TV: "Is Obama dead?"

And the following year, when a guerilla leader in Afghanistan sent squads of fanatic followers on a kamikaze mission to America, the pundit seemed to have the answer to his question. "The conventional wisdom," recalled David Axelrod, "was [that] no one named Barack Obama was going to get elected three years after 9/11."

Even so, when Republican U.S. senator Peter Fitzgerald announced he was retiring and likely Democratic candidate Jesse Jackson Jr.—a popular Illinois congressman and a friend of Obama's (Jackson's sister Santita had been a bridesmaid at Barack and Michelle's wedding)—decided against it, Obama announced his candidacy in January 2003.

As he had when he first ran for office seven years before, he first made sure the admittedly "cockeyed idea" was okay with his wife, whom he calls one of the

"You are going to be a very credible presidential candidate."

ARCHBISHOP DESMOND TUTU TO OBAMA

two "higher powers" that he consults before every major decision. Parents by then—daughter Malia was born in 1999 and her sister Sasha followed in 2001—the couple lived in a modest condo in Hyde Park, and though a two-income family, they weren't exactly rolling in money. Michelle knew the demands of campaigning, the amount of time her husband would be away, and the attention the girls wouldn't be getting from their father. Being a working mother and "the primary caregiver for two very bright

"I have chosen a life with a ridiculous schedule," wrote Obama, whose long weekends at home allowed by his Senate schedule are going to become rarer during his coming presidential campaign. Here he pitches in with the breakfast dishes before getting Malia, left, and Sasha off to school one morning in 2006.

When his family was introduced to Vice President Dick Cheney following Obama's Senate swearing-in ceremony in January 2005, daughter Malia shook the veep's hand while Sasha slapped him five.

little girls [is] crazy," she told the *New Yorker*. "It's not realistic."

She was also deeply skeptical of Obama's assurances that everything would work out. "I explained," he later told *Washingtonian*, "that what's going to happen is, I'm going to win the primary, win the general, and then I'm going to write a book."

As unlikely as that scenario must have sounded, she reluctantly agreed, but told him he "shouldn't necessarily count on her vote."

Or anyone else's for that matter. "Frankly," recalled Alabama congressman Artur Davis, "a lot of people believed that if you can't win a House seat, how are you going to win a Senate seat?"

Facing a field of six other Democratic contenders, including the Illinois state comptroller, who had the backing of Chicago's legendary Democratic Party machine as well as the state's most powerful unions and a wealthy businessman with a $29 million campaign war chest, Obama had no real organization, just a small, untried staff of four working out of a tiny office in Chicago, few interested donors, and no support from the Democratic establishment.

When he traveled downstate, he drove alone in his own car and relied on the kindness of acquaintances and friends of friends to invite a few neighbors over for a chat around the kitchen table. When he could find enough people to fill a church basement or Rotary club, he would invariably explain that his father was from Kenya, in Africa, "which is where I got the name," and his mother was from Kansas, "which is why I talk the way I do."

When he marched in Chicago's St. Patrick's Day parade, a de rigueur rite for any Illinois politician, he and the army of ten volunteers he was able to muster brought up the rear, right in front of the garbage trucks.

Most observers assumed Obama would be swept from the campaign trail along with the rest of the trash. While he might win the vote in his district and other predominately black precincts around the state, few believed he could win votes in Chicago's suburban "collar" districts or in small towns downstate where, as a *New York* magazine writer put it—wittily but unfairly as it turned out—"the typical response to a person of color was to roll up the car windows."

But the smart money hadn't reckoned on Obama's appeal to voters in the suburbs and in the small towns and farmlands of central and south Illinois, where he campaigned vigorously, drawing handfuls of farmers and

workers and shopkeepers and teachers to small coffee klatches at first, and before long, throngs. The overwhelmingly white suburbs weren't immune to Obama fever either. "Twenty years ago, if I'd said there would be lawn signs with pictures of an African American, with an African surname, all over my district on the Northwest side of Chicago,

---

"I'm not sure anybody is ready to be president before they're president."

BARACK OBAMA

---

people would have had me tested for drugs," Rahm Emanuel, a former Clinton aide who is now a congressman from Illinois, told *New York*. "Yet there they were."

"Barack's got something different," said a downstate plumber. "He makes you feel like he's not a politician, but a leader."

"I know those people," Obama said as he drove through central Illinois with a writer from the *New Yorker*. "Those are my grandparents. The food they serve is the food my grandparents served when I was growing up. Their manners, their sensibility, their sense of right and wrong— it's all totally familiar to me."

Folks took to him in such numbers that he won the primary outright with 53 percent of the vote but not before it was revealed that the ex-wife of the millionaire businessman who had been leading the field had sought a restraining order against him for striking her. Then came his general-election opponent, Jack Ryan, a conservative for whom the national Republican Party had high hopes

"Need just one ticket, willing to pay up to $75."

of winning the seat—"Six-foot-four and Hollywood handsome . . . [Ryan] keeps in moral and physical trim by going to Mass and the gym each morning," enthused conservative columnist George Will.

White hope or not, Ryan was trailing Obama by sixteen points when, to make up lost ground, he hired conservative attack-specialist Scott Howell, famous for

smearing Georgia senator Max Cleland, who had lost both legs in Vietnam, as unpatriotic and as dangerous to the nation's security as Osama bin Laden.

But Howell's tactics backfired when one of his operatives began stalking Obama with a video camera, following him everywhere and "standing less than two feet from Obama's face, barking questions," reported the Associated Press. Even Republicans were outraged. "Everybody knows politics is a contact sport," Obama said with aplomb but admitted he didn't like the intrusion, especially when the cameraman recorded him in private moments as he spoke to his wife and daughters on his cell phone. Obama turned the confrontations to his advantage however. "Scorched-earth politics," he called the tactic. "Precisely the kind of politics I want to change."

Obama walks with daughter Malia as she leaves their home in Hyde Park—a prosperous neighborhood on Chicago's South Side—on her way to school in October 2006.

Ryan's campaign eventually unraveled, and he had to drop out of the race in the midst of the tabloid scandal that erupted when his ex-wife, *Boston Public* actress Jeri Ryan, alleged in divorce papers that Will's pious Republican hero had taken her to sex clubs and tried to get her to perform public sex with him.

In the wake of the flameout, desperate Republicans imported a replacement from Maryland, the rightist former presidential candidate Alan Keyes, apparently on the theory that only another black candidate could challenge Obama. ("You know, me and you got something in common," George W. Bush would say when Obama met the president the following January. "We both had to debate Alan Keyes. That guy's a piece of work, isn't he?")

Indeed, Keyes's rants on the stump promptly alienated Illinois voters. "Saying that Jesus Christ wouldn't vote for Obama and that all gays are sinners," said one strategist, paraphrasing Keyes's typical talking points, "is beyond the bounds of acceptable speech in political debate."

If Keyes was foundering before Obama's keynote address, he stopped moving altogether after the speech. "I didn't realize that the speech would strike the chord that it did," Obama later told *Ebony*. "All I was really trying to do was describe what I was hearing on the campaign trail, the stories of the hopes, fears and struggles ordinary people are going through every day. People heard themselves in the speech and I think that made them respond."

After that it was all over but the voting. With Keyes's candidacy hopelessly behind and Obama's election virtually assured, he spent much of his time lending his newfound star power—and investing the political capital that came with it—by campaigning for other Democratic candidates around the country.

On election day he won in a landslide, with more than 70 percent of the vote and scoring pluralities in every part of the state.

With the reissue of his memoir bound for the best-seller lists, he received a $1.9 million advance for three more books. With his financial worries over, he paid off his college loans and bought a $1.6 million home for his family in Hyde Park.

In January 2005, as he and his wife arrived at a hotel in Washington days before his swearing in as the junior senator from

"I'd want to be a really great president, you know? . . . Because there are a lot of mediocre or poor presidents."

BARACK OBAMA

Illinois, Michelle remembered the prediction he had made at the beginning of the campaign when he told her his far-fetched plan to win the primary, then the election, and then write a book.

"We got off the elevator," he told *Washingtonian* magazine, "and she looked at me and said, 'I can't believe you pulled it off.'"

MAN ON THE GO

As the new star in the Democratic ranks, Sen. Barack Obama was called upon by politicians across the nation to visit their constituencies and help win votes for the party in the crucial 2006 elections. The accommodating Obama crisscrossed the nation in a dazzling display of political support, in the process gaining increased recognition for himself that will be helpful in contests to come.

Clockwise from below: Obama in Missouri with Senate candidate Claire McCaskill; in Iowa with Sen. Tom Harkin; in Ohio with gubernatorial candidate Ted Strickland; in Los Angeles for gubernatorial candidate Phil Angelides; and in Bellevue, Washington, in support of Sen. Maria Cantwell.

Clockwise from right: Obama signing books at a Philadelphia Democratic rally; in Florida with gubernatorial candidate Jim Davis; in Hoboken, New Jersey, supporting Sen. Bob Menendez; at a rally for Democratic candidates in Tempe, Arizona; in Little Rock, Arkansas, for gubernatorial candidate Mike Beebe; and in Nashville for Senate candidate Harold Ford Jr.

SENATOR OBAMA

TAKES OFF

5

For more than twenty years, the U.S. Senate's two-man Illinois delegation has hosted regular Thursday morning doughnuts-and-coffee get-togethers in the Capitol for Illinois residents who happen to be visiting Washington. The weekly Constituent Coffee meetings, a tradition begun by Illinois's popular late former senator Paul

As a member of the newly Democratic-controlled Senate Foreign Relations Committee, Obama, who takes the subway (left) to travel from his office (center) to committee meetings (right), concentrated on world affairs during his first two years in office.

Senator Obama, at work in his Chicago office, October 2, 2006.

"I do think there are moments in American history where there are opportunities to change the language of politics or set the country's sights in a different place, and I think we're in one of those moments."

BARACK OBAMA

Simon in 1985, gives regular folks a chance for an informal give-and-take with their elected officials and provides a setting for the senators to keep in touch with the voters back home.

The coffee meetings had always been friendly but subdued gatherings of seldom more than a few dozen people. But not anymore. Since Barack Obama arrived in the Capitol to more hoopla than any freshman senator in memory save Teddy and Bobby Kennedy and Hillary Clinton—

> ## "America is ready to turn the page. America is ready for a new set of challenges. This is our time. A new generation is ready to lead."
>
> BARACK OBAMA

the brothers and wife, respectively, of enormously popular former presidents—the Thursday coffee klatches were moved to a larger room in order to hold the nonetheless-overflow crowds of Obama fans, not all of them from Illinois.

Soon, Obama and Illinois's senior senator, Dick Durbin, will have to start holding the meet-and-greets in stadiums to accommodate the staff, security, and media entourage who have traveled in his wake ever since he announced his presidential candidacy. Even before then, the coffees—lively sessions in which Obama and Durbin responded to questions from constituents—had begun to seem less like informal chats around the breakfast table and more like

full-blown events where as many as one hundred and fifty people would fill the chairs, while dozens more stood in the back of the room and more still were turned away at the door. At one 2006 meeting, when Obama introduced Durbin as one of *Time* magazine's ten best senators, Durbin deferred to his younger colleague's star power, saying, "I haven't done the cover of *Newsweek* or won a Grammy."

At another Thursday coffee, Durbin reminded the crowd that after Obama had thrown out the first pitch at a Chicago White Sox game the previous year, the Sox had gone on to win the World Series for the first time in eighty-eight years. When an Illinois college student asked if he could do the same for the even-more-woeful Cubs, who will mark the one-hundredth anniversary of their last championship season in 2007, Obama said, "My arm is only so good."

Many Democrats, whose memory of their party leader's last White House residence has begun to feel almost as distant, have high hopes that Obama can work his magic for them, if not for the Cubbies.

After his swearing-in to the Senate on a bright and warm winter day in January 2005, with his wife and children and family members from Hawaii and Kenya proudly looking on, Obama attended a reception in the East Room of the White House. As he walked through the crowd of mostly Republican congressional newcomers, a photographer asked a reporter standing nearby, "Who is that guy?" Without waiting for an answer, he added, "He's certainly got 'It.'"

"The Natural," *The Atlantic Monthly* called him a little less than two years later,

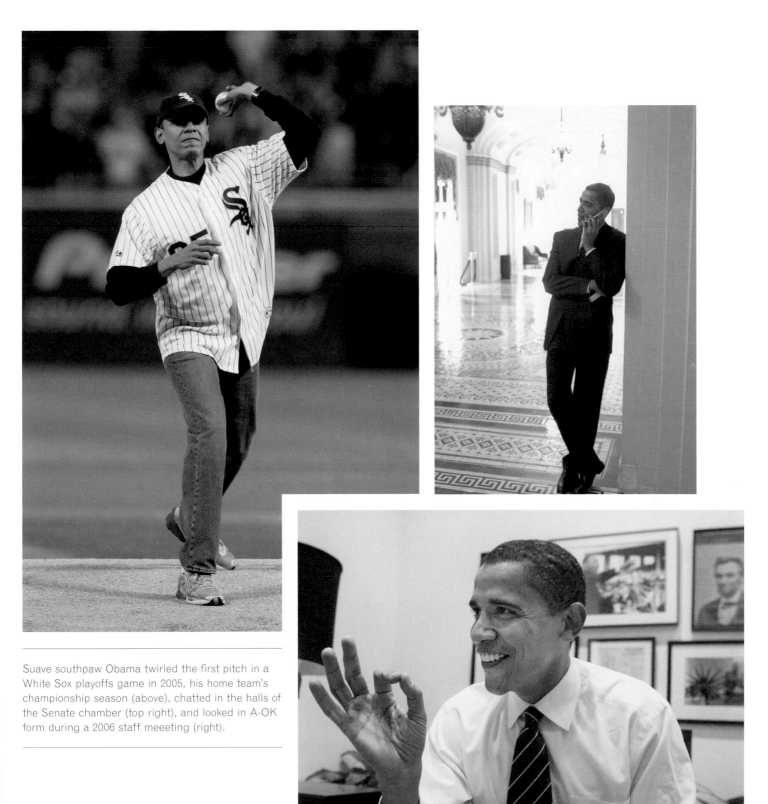

Suave southpaw Obama twirled the first pitch in a White Sox playoffs game in 2005, his home team's championship season (above), chatted in the halls of the Senate chamber (top right), and looked in A-OK form during a 2006 staff meeeting (right).

following the 2006 midterm elections when Obama's stumping for Democrats helped sweep them back into power and he was hailed as the bright, vigorous, young star of the newly resurgent party. "Obama has already established himself as the paramount leader of the next generation," declared one Democratic power broker. "There's no one even close."

Britain's *New Statesman* called him one of ten people "who could change the

"If you were my husband, I wouldn't let you go around alone."

FEMALE GUEST AT A ILLINOIS DENTAL SOCIETY DINNER TO OBAMA

world." The online magazine *Slate* dropped the qualifier: Obama already had "turned American politics upside down."

The site's editor, Jacob Weisberg, was speaking with urgency about an event then still two years in the future—the 2008 presidential elections. A short while before,

New York senator Hillary Clinton, who hadn't yet declared her candidacy for her party's nomination, was nonetheless widely regarded as the Democrat to beat. Not so fast, said Weisberg. Obama, he wrote, "not Hillary [would] be the de facto Democratic front-runner" should he join the race.

When, in December 2006, Obama confessed that he was considering just such a course, the possibility of his candidacy became the talk of the republic. Oprah, Larry King, and Jay Leno lined up to get him to announce on their shows. "If Obama runs, he wins," posted Markos Moulitsas of the liberal blog *Daily Kos*.

When Charlie Rose asked guest Nora Ephron—a Washington insider once married to *Washington Post* journalist Carl Bernstein—who was on air to plug her book *I Feel Bad About My Neck* if she thought Obama was ready for the job, Ephron made it clear she liked him better than she liked her own body parts. "I don't want to wait until he is ready," said the screenwriter whose films *Sleepless in Seattle* and *When Harry Met Sally . . .* demonstrated her acute

A persuasive speaker, Obama (meeting with a student group in 2006) disarmed a skeptical audience during a speech on Israel. "[H]e was incredibly thoughtful," said one audience member. "And the crowd was just wowed. Barack managed to make those people who disagreed with him feel comfortable with the disagreement."

> ## "If there's a child on the South Side of Chicago that can't read, that makes a difference in my life, even if it's not my child."
>
> BARACK OBAMA

sense of the zeitgeist. "I'm ready for Barack Obama. I don't think we have six years to wait for him, because things are going to hell in a handbasket."

Democrats weren't alone in seeing Obama as a formidable candidate. "In Republican circles," said a former fellow Illinois state senator, "we've always feared that Barack would become a rock star of American politics."

"Barack Obama is a walking, talking hope machine," said Texas Republican Mark McKinnon, who has worked as an aide to George W. Bush. "People see him as a reflection about what is good and great about America. He's like a mirror of what people think we ought to be. He is

Three presidents? Obama flew to Houston following Hurricane Katrina with Bill Clinton and George H. W. Bush to speak with displaced New Orleans residents in September 2005. In the Senate, he cosponsored a bill to stop the second Bush administration from awarding no-bid reconstruction contracts.

cosponsored a number of bills, including one that passed in both houses of Congress to create a public Internet site that enables taxpayers to track how the government spends their money. They also joined forces in the wake of Hurricane Katrina

successful, talented, respectful, moderate, judicious, thoughtful, and deeply human."

McKinnon went so far as to coin a potential Obama slogan. "I think people see him as a human bridge that can unite the country," he wrote in an e-mail to a reporter, dubbing the possible President Obama the "healer-in-chief."

Even Bush's Director of Strategic Initiatives, Peter Wehner, applauded the senator-author's call to stop all the bitter bickering and come together to get things done for the good of the country: "Barack Obama comes across as reasonable, civil, above-the-fray, well intentioned, fair-minded, non-ideological, agreeable."

Obama earned these kind of kudos from the opposite side in his first two years in the Republican-controlled Senate, just as he did as a progressive, minority-party state senator in Springfield. "If Barack disagrees with you or thinks you haven't done something appropriate," said Oklahoma's Tom Coburn, one of the most conservative Republicans in the Senate, "he's the kind of guy who'll talk to you about it. He'll come up and reconcile: 'I don't think you were truthful about my bill.' I've seen him do that. On the Senate floor."

Coburn and Obama struck up a friendship when they both arrived in Washington in 2005 as incoming senators. The two socialize, conduct brainstorming sessions during informal dinners, and have

"I am just very impressed with him as a man, as a lawyer, as an individual, and as someone who chose not to go to a law firm but to be a community organizer and to do something about community problems."

VERNON JORDAN, OBAMA FRIEND AND
CLINTON ADMINISTRATION ADVISOR

to stop the Bush administration from funneling taxpayer money to hand-picked companies by awarding no-bid contracts for reconstruction projects in the ravaged Gulf Coast.

At least some of Obama's bipartisan appeal, noted *The Nation*, stems from the realization of Republicans that Obama's star power will enhance any bill he cosponsors with them. But Coburn, for one, genuinely believes that Obama transcends party lines in a way that a true statesman should.

"What Washington does," Coburn said in *Harper's* last year, sounding very much like he read the galleys of Obama's latest book, "is cause everybody to concentrate on where they disagree as opposed to where

Baseball was one subject George W. Bush and Obama (with Sen. Dick Durbin, left, and White Sox owner Jerry Reinsdorf, right, following a salute to the 2005 World Series winners) saw eye to eye on.

they agree. But leadership changes that. And Barack's got the capability, I believe—and the pizzazz and the charisma—to be a leader of America, not a leader of Democrats."

There are plenty who think Obama can lead the party straight back to the White House. Former Senate Minority Leader Tom Daschle, now a political consultant in Washington, sees Obama as a rising star

them 'overnight sensations.' But he worked to get to this point. There is nothing 'overnight' about Barack Obama."

Other Democrats were almost giddy in anticipation of him running. Calling him "the first post-ideological candidate," Rahm Emanuel, the Illinois congressman and powerful Democratic national strategist, said he thinks "Barack could be a player in all fifty states . . . There are states we have lost, historically, that he'd be a major player in."

"We must understand that the might of our military has to be matched by the strength of our diplomacy."

BARACK OBAMA

For out-of-power Democrats, particularly progressives who had all but given up on the social, economic, and foreign policy reforms they long for, Obama's appeal is almost intoxicating. "When you do political stuff and you run into a Barack," said Judd Miner, a partner in Obama's civil rights law firm and an aide in his Senate campaign, "you think, 'Oh, there's hope!'"

A similar kind of recognition can inspire the armies of activist volunteers essential to a successful presidential campaign. "People call it drinking the juice," said Dan Shomon, who as political director of Obama's Senate campaign helped marshall his candidate's eager supporters to canvas neighborhoods, distribute literature, work phone banks, and drive voters to the polls. "People start drinking the Obama juice [and] you can't find enough for them to do."

the Democrats might do well to attach their aspirations to. Impressed as everyone with Obama's charisma as a candidate—"he has got as much of it as anybody I know"—Daschle said, "Obama is the real thing. He has grown in stature in so many different ways in the short time that he has appeared on the public scene. He's a rising star, like a lot of people in other walks of life. We call

But some Democrats wonder if the Obama high is good for the party. Where there are many who compare Obama to successful charismatic candidates of the past ("He awakens that JFK appeal of a candidate who is young, attractive, and brainy," said Princeton presidential scholar Fred Greenstein) others say Kennedy's war service and experience—he won Navy and Marine Corps medals for heroism in the Pacific and was twice elected to the Senate and served eight years before entering the White House in 1961—made him more qualified than Obama, who they note has gone through the fire of only a single Senate race and will have served only four years by 2009, when the next administration begins.

Supporters point out that Obama will be forty-nine by then (JFK was only forty-three when he ran in 1960) and that his critics discount the seven years he spent in the Illinois legislature. And, they add,

---

"War hero against snot-nosed rookie."

BARACK OBAMA, ON A POSSIBLE SOUNDBITE
FOR A McCAIN-OBAMA PRESIDENTIAL RACE

---

the current president served a single term as governor in a state where the legislature has more power than the executive branch and prepared for political office by running a failed oil-drilling company and serving as partial owner of a baseball team, while Obama toiled for years helping the poor and disenfranchised as a community organizer and civil rights attorney.

"The important thing is not experience per se—Donald Rumsfeld and Dick Cheney had the best résumés in Washington and initiated a fiasco in Iraq," Obama said last year, "but rather, does someone have the judgment necessary to learn from experience and make good decisions?"

"It's not experience that people are demanding," Republican pollster Frank Luntz told the *National Journal.* "It's capability. It's not 'have you done it before?' It's 'could you do it in the future?' And Obama has that 'could-do-it' image."

"People want confidence that a president will lead and have strong convictions and integrity," added former Bill Clinton Press Secretary Mike McCurry. "Senator Obama exudes all that out of every pore."

Other critics question Obama's electability in the Democratic primary, much less the general election against as formidable an opponent as the likely Republican front-runner John McCain, the four-term senator and decorated former Vietnam POW whose medals in a time of war—even one as unpopular as the disastrous one in Iraq—will shine all the more.

Supporters say Obama's comparative youth will work in his favor. He's twenty-five years younger than McCain, eighteen years younger than John Kerry, thirteen years younger than Hillary Clinton and Al Gore, and eight years younger than John Edwards, all potential candidates. "There's something to be said," Jennifer Senior wrote in a good-humored and insightful article in *New York* about Obama's post–baby boomer appeal, "for a politician who didn't come of age wearing sideburns and listening to Simon and Garfunkel."

Obama himself sees his youth as an advantage with an electorate that, he told Senior, has tired of leaders arguing over old issues. "These are fights that were taking place back in dorm rooms in the sixties," he said, alluding to so-called culture war squabbles over issues like Vietnam and sexual freedom. "I think people feel like, 'Okay, let's not re-litigate the sixties forty years later.'"

Even an Obama critic like *New York*'s John Heilemann agrees: "The essence of Obama's pitch is that it's time to move past the old politics and that he's the embodiment of the new. And after the scorched-earth tactics and wretched polarization of the Clinton-Bush years, anyone who dismisses the potency of that message hasn't been paying attention."

But Heilemann also points out that much of the enthusiasm for Obama is based on the notion that he is simply not Hilary Clinton, whom many regard as a strong candidate to win the Democratic nomination but who, as a writer in the *National Journal* put it, would be "likely cannon fodder in the general election." As a political strategist told the magazine: "There's great fear in Democratic circles that . . . in the general election [Senator Clinton] cannot win. The thirst for a new

Combining business and pleasure, Obama met with Archbishop Desmond Tutu during a fact-finding visit to South Africa and Kenya, where he spoke on the AIDS and Darfur crises and scolded the Kenyan government for human-rights abuses and restricting civil rights in a nationally televised speech in August 2006.

face is palpable. I hear it in almost every political conversation with a Democrat."

At the same time, Heilemann wrote, "What Obama has going for him that Hillary does not is that people genuinely like him. The power of personality in politics cannot

---

"He may not have forty years in politics, but he's not exactly a child here. He's a well-established guy who knows a lot about the world."

WILLIAM M. DALEY, FORMER U.S. SECRETARY OF COMMERCE, ON OBAMA

---

be overstated." Even so, he added, "Hillary Clinton remains the prohibitive favorite to win the Democratic nomination. She has the money. She has the résumé. She has the policy chops, the shrewdest political adviser on the planet (i.e., her husband), and the unwavering allegiance of a substantial bloc of her party's primary voters."

And Heilemann is among those who say Obama could wither in the heat of the general-election campaign. As a Democratic strategist in that camp said of Obama, "He's never been tested, never been scrutinized. There's never been anyone who's pored through his past the way the Republicans will. He would be a stronger candidate if he had gone through that crucible of fire."

Obama agreed as much, telling a reporter that because his Republican opponent dropped out of the race before his newly hired attack specialist could formulate an effective strategy, "I sort of got a free pass

. . . I wasn't subjected to a bunch of negative ads. And nobody thought I was going to win. So I basically got into the habit of pretty much saying what I thought. And it worked for me. So I figured I might as well keep on doing it."

But in anticipation of just such attacks, his own campaign pored over his state senate record to find the kind of information the Republicans might use against him. His researchers, he writes in *Audacity*, "didn't find a lot, but they found enough to do the trick—a dozen or so votes that, if described without context, could be made to sound pretty scary."

One was a drug-crimes bill "so poorly drafted that I concluded it was both ineffective and unconstitutional." Obama voted against it, leaving him open to an attack ad like one his research staff suggested the Republicans might use: "Obama voted to weaken penalties on gang-bangers who deal drugs in schools." Another claimed he had voted against a bill to "protect our children from sex offenders." Obama protested that he pressed the nay rather than the aye button by mistake and had the vote quickly corrected in the official record. "Somehow I don't think that portion of the official record will make it into a Republican ad," his campaign manager, David Axelrod, said with a wry smile.

As for his short tenure in the U.S. Senate, Obama is well aware that researchers working not only for Republicans but for Democrats as well are already looking through his voting record for mud to sling. Most political analysts agree that one of the reasons only two sitting senators—Warren

The day after Obama and his wife took AIDS tests (right) in Kisumu, Kenya, to dispel local fears that have slowed progress in fighting the disease, he posed with a high-minded observer near the Somalia border in August 2005.

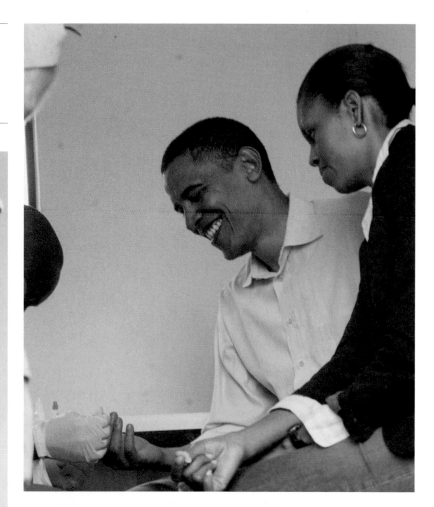

"In a country of 300 million people," Obama told an interviewer in his Senate office after the 2006 midterm elections, "there is a certain degree of audacity required for anybody to say I'm the best person to lead this country."

G. Harding and John F. Kennedy—have ever been elected president since 1900 is that their voting records provide much fertile ground for such searches.

In a wonderfully anecdotal and insightful chapter in his book about the history and inner workings of the Senate, Obama quotes a passage from Kennedy's *Profiles in Courage* about "the dread finality of decision that confronts a senator facing an important call of the roll.

"He may want more time for his decision," Kennedy wrote, "he may believe there is something to be said for both sides—he may feel that a slight amendment could remove all difficulties—but when that roll is called he cannot hide, he cannot equivocate, he cannot delay."

Ranked ninety-ninth in seniority in the one-hundred-seat Senate, Obama was careful during his freshman year to not allow his star power to intrude on the chamber. "He doesn't want to be this messianic figure carrying stone tablets," Axelrod told a reporter. "He understands he has to do the work." Said Michelle Obama: "I see my husband rolling up his sleeves and finally doing something to warrant all of this attention."

For Obama, getting down to work meant politely turning down some three hundred invitations per week to speak or appear on talk shows and at public events. Instead he kept a low profile and concentrated on hiring staff (including Daschle's former

chief of staff), making friends on both sides of the aisle, and conferring with elders like Ted Kennedy, Robert C. Byrd—the ninetyish long-ago member of the Raleigh County (West Virginia) Ku Klux Klan, with whom he formed a close bond—and, yes, Hillary Clinton. He also focused on nuts-and-bolts issues like veterans' disability and federal infrastructure spending, which were of concern to the folks back home, and bills scheduled to come up for any of JFK's unforgiving roll calls.

Just two weeks into his term, one of those roll-call votes put him on the outs with his own party and some of his biggest campaign contributors. Obama voted with Republicans

> **"Our leaders in Washington seem incapable of working together in a practical, common-sense way. Politics has become so bitter and partisan, so gummed up by money and influence, that we can't tackle the big problems that demand solutions."**
>
> BARACK OBAMA

on a bill to limit class-action lawsuits, alienating the consumer, labor, and civil rights groups that supported him, not to mention lawyer groups that had contributed heavily to his campaign. "When multimillion-dollar settlements are handed down and all the victims get are coupons for a free product, justice is not being served," Obama, who believes such suits should be heard in state or federal—not local—courts, said in a statement explaining his vote. "And when cases are tried in counties only because it's known that those judges will award big payoffs, you get quick settlements without ever finding out who's right and who's wrong."

"Are you going to try to be president? Shouldn't you be vice president first?"

After Todd Smith, the president of the Association of Trial Lawyers of America, one of Obama's contributors and a major force behind the bill he voted against, visited him to express his disappointment, the lobbyist told *American Prospect* magazine that his group's political action committee would continue to contribute to Obama's campaigns. "It was quite open," Smith said. "He said, 'Todd, go right ahead, speak your mind.' And I did. He believed there needed to be changes and . . . he felt [his vote] was the right way to go. I don't think your support for somebody rises or falls on a single issue. He will be there for regular people and their rights the vast majority of the time, and when he's not, it's going to be—at least in his mind, I'm certain—for solid reasons. He's an outstanding U.S. senator already."

While he has sided with his party in most votes, including those on Bush's Supreme Court nominees (he voted nay), stem-cell research (aye), and an amendment to the

"It's very difficult to think about something as massive as running for president at this time," Michelle (with her family in Hyde Park, above) said in March 2006. "That is not a part of our day-to-day conversation." Apparently it was by December, when Obama spoke in New Hampshire, a month before he launched his campaign for the White House (right).

"I personally have high hopes for him."

HAROLD M. ICKES, HILLARY CLINTON SENATE CAMPAIGN ADVISOR, ON OBAMA

"Hillary Clinton can't match Obama's rhetorical skills and often doesn't come across well in larger groups," wrote one commentator about Obama (with Clinton at the 2006 NAACP convention, below; and campaigning for Illinois Iraq war veteran Tammy Duckworth, right). "She wins over smaller groups and individuals one-on-one. Obama is the master of the large group."

constitution to outlaw flag-burning (nay), he angered party liberals by modifying his previously strong antiwar position after repeated visits to the country on fact-finding trips during his first two years in office.

Though he still thinks the invasion was a disastrous mistake, opposes Bush's recent "surge" in troop levels, and calls for an immediate redeployment to prevent American soldiers from being caught in the cross fire of a bloody sectarian civil war, in 2006 when Democratic congressman John Murtha called for immediate withdrawal, Obama spoke to the Chicago Council on Foreign Relations, saying among other things that the United States must "manage our exit in a responsible way—with the hope of leaving a stable foundation for the future."

Washington Post columnist David Broder praised Obama for finding a "sensible common ground" and pointing "the administration and the country toward a realistic and modestly hopeful course on Iraq."

On other issues too he has tried to take a fresh look at old conundrums that the Democrats have long wrestled with. "Sometimes," he said last year of the Republican lock on votes from the Christian Right, "the Democratic Party, I think, just assumes that as long as people are in church that somehow we can't reach them, that we have nothing in common. That's simply not true and certainly hasn't been true historically." And as for the Christian Coalition and other politically active religious groups, he said "religious folks need to understand that separation of church and state isn't there just to protect the state from religion, but religion from the state."

When he appealed to union groups to accept globalization as a fact of life during

"There's an optimism and lack of anger," New Jersey governor Jon Corzine said of Obama (carrying Thanksgiving groceries for a food-bank client, below; and visiting Nelson Mandela's former jail cell in Cape Town in 2006, right). "There is a reach for a positive framing of even negative issues."

"One thing I'm convinced of is that people want something new."

BARACK OBAMA

Sharp ears to go with the silver tongue: As he did at a forum in Boston (above), Obama listened carefully at a meeting of Illinois nuclear weapons plant workers (right, in 2006) and then spoke for their cause before the Federal Advisory Board on Radiation and Worker Health.

his Senate campaign *New Yorker* writer William Finnegan asked him if he wasn't, "waving a red flag in front of labor."

Obama replied: "Look, those guys are all wearing Nike shoes and buying Pioneer stereos. They don't want the borders closed. They just don't want their communities destroyed."

On universal health care, Obama said that Democrats had not pushed hard enough for fear of being attacked as "'tax-and-spend liberals.' But that's not a good reason to not do something," he said. "You don't give up on the goal of universal health care because you don't want to be tagged as a liberal. People need universal health care."

"To me," he told one reporter, "the issue is not, Are you centrist or are you liberal? The issue to me is, Is what you're proposing going to work? Can you build a working coalition to make the lives of people better? And if it can work, you should support it whether it's centrist, conservative, or liberal."

In another interview, Obama described himself as a politician whose "values are deeply rooted in the progressive tradition, the values of equal opportunity, civil rights, fighting for working families, a foreign policy that is mindful of human rights, a strong belief in civil liberties, wanting to be a good steward for the environment, a sense that the government has an important role to play, that opportunity is open to all people, and that the powerful don't trample on the less powerful."

As for his ability to convey his vision to the electorate, Obama has no doubt. "I feel confident that if you put me in a room with anybody—black, white, Hispanic, Republican, Democrat—give me half an hour and I will walk out with the votes of most of the folks," he told *Newsweek*. "I don't feel constrained by race, geography, or background in terms of making a connection with people."

Maintaining that connection is one of the things Obama loves most about politics. He has hosted more than forty town meetings in Illinois since his term in

Washington began. In the sessions, convened in high schools, on college campuses, or in libraries in towns and cities across the state, Obama takes questions and, he writes in *Audacity*, "I answer to the people who sent me to Washington . . . They ask me about prescription drugs, the deficit, human rights in Myanmar, ethanol, bird flu, school funding, and the space program . . . And as I look out over the crowd, I somehow feel encouraged. In their bearing I see hard work. In the way they handle their children

"We need to take faith seriously not simply to block the religious right but to engage all persons of faith in the larger project of American renewal."

BARACK OBAMA

"The Land of Lincoln Loves Senator Obama."

SIGN OBSERVED AT AN ILLINOIS AFL-CIO MEETING

"Obama!" George W. Bush said at a 2005 White House reception the day before his swearing-in to the Senate. "Come and meet Laura. Laura, you remember Obama. We saw him on TV during election night." Obama (at the White House, above; getting the kids to school in Chicago, right; and on the road, inset) recounts the scene in his book: After shaking hands, "The president turned to an aide nearby, who squirted a big dollop of hand sanitizer in the president's hand." At upper right Michelle speaks to a high school economics class in Elmhurst, Illinois.

I see hope. My time with them is like a dip in a cool stream. I feel cleansed afterward, glad for the work I have chosen."

The thing Obama likes least about Washington is that it's not home—not yet anyway. Arranging his schedule so that he can fly back to Chicago on Thursday nights, spending the weekend with his family and returning to Washington on Mondays, he

does his best to help his wife, who runs the University of Chicago Hospitals' ambitious community relations and diversity programs, as well as the Obama household.

While Obama pitches in as best he can to see that their daughters, Malia and Sasha, get to school and home in time for piano and ballet classes and homework, Michelle, whom *Ebony* magazine dubbed "the quintessential working Sister," admits, as she did to the *New Yorker*'s William Finnegan, that the lot of the political wife is "hard. And that's why Barack is such a grateful man."

When Obama was elected to the Senate, he and Michelle agreed that she and the children would remain in Chicago where

"It's paparazzi. Stop looking at it."

BARACK OBAMA TO REPORTERS TEASING HIM ABOUT SWIMSUIT PHOTOS

Surfin' U.S.A.: On a beachin' day in Hawaii, Barack Obama got tubular as a tyke (far left); years later, he boogie-boarded with his own kids on a Hawaii vacation during the Christmas holidays of 2006. Just a few weeks later, he revealed that he was going to try to catch a wave that his supporters hope will leave him sittin' on top of the world.

"The euphoria is explosive. We have been so hopeless for the last six years."

MIKE HUXTABLE OF PORTSMOUTH, NEW HAMPSHIRE, WAITING TO SEE OBAMA

"Barack is the most unique political talent I've run into in more than fifty years," said one lifelong Democrat who, like many Obama supporters (at a New Hampshire book-signing in December 2006, top, where buttons were available for sale, above), says he will be a formidable campaigner. "He has the ability to touch diverse crowds," said one, "and there's a sense of clicking."

she has a large support group, with her mother and brother (her father died before she and Obama married), relations and friends all living nearby. "I have a big village here," Michelle told *Ebony*. "Unless it was absolutely necessary, we felt it would just be good to stay close to our base. It's proven to be a smart move, and [Barack's] come to understand the wisdom of my plan."

When he arrives from Washington, Obama has to check his superstardom at the door. "Giving a good speech doesn't make you Superman," Michelle told a reporter following his 2004 Democratic Convention keynote address. And she hasn't been shy about pointing out to reporters that he stays up late, doesn't make his bed, and leaves dirty socks on the floor, and she makes no secret of her disapproval of his smoking, a lifelong on-and-off habit that he had managed to kick for a time but resumed during the stress of the Senate campaign.

Even from afar, she makes sure he keeps things in perspective. When he telephoned her from the Capitol to share news of a breakthrough he scored on the Senate Foreign Relations Committee for a bill he was cosponsoring to restrict black-market arms trade, she interrupted him, he recounts in *The Audacity of Hope*, as he was enthusing about his legislative triumph.

"'We have ants.'

"'Huh?'

"'I found ants in the kitchen. And in the bathroom upstairs . . . I need you to buy some ant traps on your way home tomorrow.'"

"I hung up the receiver," Obama writes, "wondering if Ted Kennedy or John McCain bought ant traps on the way home from work."

Obama stays in a one-bedroom rented apartment on Massachusetts Avenue and seldom attends the Capitol's glitzier social events when he's in Washington, preferring to join colleagues for bull sessions over beers or steak dinners, discussing, no doubt, politics. ("You've got at least eight Democrats running for the presidency," he mused to a reporter last year. "I'd say we're gonna have some silly season goin' on.")

To relax, he watches ball games on TV and works out at the Senate gym. Often, in the evenings, he jogs to the Washington Monument and sometimes continues on to the Lincoln Memorial and up the stairs to stand at the spot where Martin Luther King Jr. gave his "I Have a Dream" speech in 1963, the Capitol dome shining in the distance.

"And in that place, I think about America and those who built it," he writes in the closing passages of *The Audacity of Hope*. "And those like Lincoln and King, who ultimately laid down their lives in the service of perfecting an imperfect union . . . It is that process I wish to be part of.

"My heart is filled with love for this country."

In Swahili, his father's language, Barack means "blessing" or "blessing from God." In Hebrew, it means "flash of lightning."

Whichever Barack Obama proves to be—destined for the White House, or a bolt that lights the skies momentarily—the image he leaves, lasting or fleeting, will be one of hope, idealism, and faith in the promise of America.

"He realizes that this is his time."

FORMER SENATOR BOB KERREY ON OBAMA

Page 6: Reuters/Kevin Lamarque/Landov

Pages 8-9: AP/M. Spencer Green (left); Aurora Photos/ Samantha Appleton (center); AP/M. Spencer Green (top right)

Pages 10-11: Reuters/Mike Segar/Landov (left); AP/Charlie Neibergall (center); AP/Ron Edmonds (right)

Pages 12-13: AP/Chicago Tribune/Nancy Stone (top left); Reuters/John Gress/Landov (bottom left); AP/Susan Walsh (center)

Pages 14-15: AP/J. Scott Applewhite (left inset); Reuters/John Gress/Landov

Pages 16-17: AP/Jeff Roberson

Pages 18-19: AP/Kiichiro Sato (left); AP/Rob Carr (right)

Pages 20-21: AP/Evan Vucci

Page 22: UPI/Roger L. Wollenberg/Landov

Pages 24-25: AP/Michael A. Mariant (bottom left); AP/ Mannie Garcia (center); Reuters/Fred Prouser/Landov (upper right); UPI/Dennis Brack/Landov (bottom right)

Page 26: AP/M. Spencer Green

Page 29: AP/Nam Y. Huh

Pages 30-31: AP/Manuel Balce Ceneta (bottom left); Aurora Photos/Callie Shell (top left); AP/Pablo Martinez Monsivais (bottom right)

Page 33: AP/Manuel Balce Ceneta (top); Aurora Photos/Callie Shell (bottom right)

Page 35: UPI/Brendan Smialowski/Landov

Pages 36-37: AP/Sayyid Azim (left); Reuters/Radu Sigheti/ Landov (center); AP/Sayyid Azim (top right)

Page 38: Reuters/Radu Sigheti/Landov (bottom left); AP/ Sayyid Azim

Pages 40-41: Jeff Widener

Page 42: Polaris

Pages 44-45: Associated Press (left); Polaris (right)

Pages 46-50: Jeff Widener

Page 52: Associated Press

Pages 54-59: Jeff Widener

Pages 60-61: Joseph White (left); AP/Tina Fineberg (top left); Bloomberg News/Jennifer S. Altman/Landov (center)

Pages 64-65: AP/M. Spencer Green

Page 67: AP/Nam Y. Huh

Pages 68-69: Polaris (left); AP/Sayyid Azim (center); AP/Karel Prinsloo (bottom right)

Pages 72-73: AP/Chitose Suzuki (top left); Polaris (center and right)

Pages 74-75: AP/Ron Edmonds (left); Newhouse News Service/Landov (top right); AP/Steve Matteo (right)

Page 76: AP/Charlie Neibergall (top); AP/Ed Reinke (bottom)

Pages 78-79: AP/M. Spencer Green

Page 80: AP/M. Spencer Green (top left); AP/State Journal Register/Kevin German (bottom right)

Pages 82-83: AP/Jeff Roberson (left inset); Aurora Photos/ Samantha Appleton (center and bottom right)

Page 84: AP/M. Spencer Green

Pages 86-87: Aurora Photos/Callie Shell

Page 88: UPI/Michael Kleinfeld/Landov

Page 90: Aurora Photos/Callie Shell

Pages 92-93: Clockwise from top center: AP/Charlie Riedel; AP/Charlie Neibergall; AP/Kiichiro Sato; Reuters/Lucy Nicholson/Landov; AP/Elaine Thompson

Pages 94-95: Clockwise from top center: AP/Tom Mihalek; AP/Alan Diaz; AP/Mike Derer; AP/Paul Connors; AP/Ron Ira Steele; AP/Alex Brandon

Pages 96-97: Aurora Photos/Callie Shell (left inset and center); AP/Gerald Herbert (right inset)

Pages 98-99: Aurora Photos/Callie Shell

Page 101: AP/Ann Heisenfelt (top left); UPI/Roger L. Wollenberg/Landov (top right); AP/Manuel Balce Ceneta (bottom right)

Pages 102-103: AP/Manuel Balce Ceneta

Page 104: AP/Richard Carson

Pages 106-107: AP/Pablo Martinez Monsivais

Page 109: AP/Obed Zilwa

Page 111: AP/Sayyid Azim (top right); Reuters/Daud Yussuf/ Landov (left)

Page 112: AP/Pablo Martinez Monsivais

Pages 114-115: Aurora Photos/Callie Shell (top); AP/Jim Cole (bottom)

Pages 116-117: AP/Evan Vucci (left); AP/M. Spencer Green (right)

Pages 118-119: AP/M. Spencer Green (bottom left); Reuters/ Howard Burditt/Landov (top right)

Pages 120-121: AP/Steven Senne (top left); AP/Brian Kersey (bottom right)

Pages 122-123: Clockwise from left: UPI/Roger L. Wollenberg/Landov; AP/Jeff Roberson; AP/Jim Cole; Aurora Photos/Callie Shell

Pages 124-125: Polaris (left inset); Fame Pictures (center, top right, bottom right)

Pages 126-127: AP/Jim Cole (top left); Reuters/Brian Snyder/ Landov (bottom left); AP/Seth Wenig (right)

Back cover photos: clockwise from top left: UPI/Dennis Brack/Landov; AP/M. Spencer Green; AP/Seth Wenig; AP/Charlie Neibergall; AP/Gerald Herbert; AP/Evan Vucci; AP/Nam Y. Huh; Reuters/Brian Snyder/Landov